Edmund Wilson Revisited

Twayne's United States Authors Series

Frank Day, Editor

Clemson University

TUSAS 695

Edmund Wilson Revisited

David Castronovo

Twayne Publishers
An Imprint of Simon & Schuster Macmillan
New York

Prentice Hall International
London • Mexico City • New Delhi • Singapore • Sydney • Toronto

Jacket photograph © 1975 Richard Avedon. All rights reserved.

Twayne's United States Authors Series No. 695

Edmund Wilson Revisited
David Castronovo

Twayne Publishers
An Imprint of Simon & Schuster Macmillan
1633 Broadway
New York, NY 10019

Library of Congress Cataloging-in-Publication Data

Castronovo, David.
    Edmund Wilson revisited / David Castronovo.
        p.   cm. — (Twayne's United States authors series ; TUSAS 695)
    Includes bibliographical references and index.
    ISBN 0-8057-1642-4 (alk. paper)
    1. Wilson, Edmund, 1895–1972—Criticism and interpretation.
    2. Wilson, Edmund, 1895–1972—Knowledge—Literature.   3. Criticism—
United States—History—20th century.   I. Title.   II. Series.
PS3545.I6245Z587   1998
818'.5209—dc21   97-31613
                                                                                                          CIP

This paper meets the requirements of ANSI/NISO Z3948–1992 Permanence of Paper.

10 9 8 7 6 5 4 3 2 1

Printed in the United States of America

For D.L.C.

Contents

Chronology

1895   Edmund Wilson Jr. is born on May 8 in Red Bank, New Jersey, to Edmund and Helen Mather (Kimball) Wilson.

1908   Travels to Europe. Enters Hill School in Pottstown, Pennsylvania; writes for Hill *Record* during his years as a student; studies with Rolfe.

1912   Graduates from Hill; enters Princeton University; studies with Gauss; friendship with F. Scott Fitzgerald and John Peale Bishop; writes for *Nassau Literary Magazine*.

1916   Graduates from Princeton. Goes for summer to military preparedness camp in Plattsburgh, New York. Soon becomes a reporter for New York *Evening Sun*.

1917   Serves with military hospital unit; attends wounded in Vosges, France.

1918   Through father's influence, changes to Intelligence Corps in Chaumont.

1919   Returns to New York and is demobilized; works at freelance writing.

1920   Works as managing editor of *Vanity Fair*. Meets Edna Millay.

1921   Becomes managing editor of the *New Republic* (February); travels to Europe (March).

1922   *The Undertaker's Garland,* written in collaboration with John Peale Bishop, published; returns to *Vanity Fair,* again as managing editor, July to May 1923.

1923   Marries Mary Blair, an actress; father dies in May; first child, Rosalind, is born.

1924   *The Crime in the Whistler Room* produced by Provincetown Players starring Mary Blair.

1925   Separates from Mary Blair.

1926   *Discordant Encounters* published.

1927   Stays in Provincetown and Boston during summer. Begins work on *Axel's Castle*.

1928   Works on *I Thought of Daisy* and *Axel's Castle*.

1929   *I Thought of Daisy* and *Poet's Farewell!* published. Suffers nervous breakdown in March, goes to a sanitarium in Clifton Springs, New York; briefly addicted to paraldehyde; divorced from Mary Blair.

1930   "Politically I am going further and further toward the left." Marries Margaret Canby, a Californian.

1931   *Axel's Castle* published. Works on "a book" about the crisis in America.

1932   *The American Jitters* (later "The Earthquake" section of *The American Earthquake*) published; Margaret Canby dies from a fall in California.

1933   Works at the *New Republic*.

1934   Works on Marx and Vico; the *New Republic;* publishes first chapters of *To the Finland Station*.

1935   Travels to Russia from May to October on Guggenheim Fellowship.

1936   Publishes *Travels in Two Democracies* (American portion to appear later in *The American Earthquake*).

1937   *This Room and This Gin and These Sandwiches,* a collection of plays, published.

1938   *The Triple Thinkers,* first edition, published. Marries Mary McCarthy in April; son, Reuel Kimball Wilson, born on Christmas Day; works on *The Wound and the Bow*.

1939   Teaches in summer session at University of Chicago.

1940   *To the Finland Station* published; begins correspondence and friendship with Vladimir Nabokov.

1941   *The Boys in the Back Room* and *The Wound and the Bow* published; in the spring he stops "working in the office" at the *New Republic* as a result of a disagreement about the war.

1942   *Notebooks of Night* published; lectures at Smith College.

1943–1944   Works as a book reviewer for *The New Yorker*.

1945 *"The New Yorker* is sending me to Europe."

1946 *Memoirs of Hecate County* published. Divorces Mary McCarthy. Marries Elena Thornton Mumm.

1947 *Europe Without Baedeker* published; travels to New Mexico for *The New Yorker.*

1948 Third child, Helen Miranda Wilson, born in February.

1949 *The Reporter* sends Wilson to Haiti.

1950 *Classics and Commercials* published; begins going to Talcottville during summer.

1951 Wilson's mother dies in March; *The Little Blue Light* produced in April by ANTA; Christian Gauss dies at Princeton.

1952 *The Shores of Light* published.

1954 *Five Plays* published; *"The New Yorker* is sending me to Israel."

1955 *The Scrolls from the Dead Sea* (later published with *Israel*); receives gold medal from American Academy of Arts and Letters.

1956 Honorary degree from Princeton; beginning of attempts to deal with tax problems; *Red, Black, Blond and Olive* and *A Piece of My Mind* published.

1957 Writes about the Iroquois for *The New Yorker.*

1958 *The American Earthquake* published.

1959–1960 Accepts Lowell lectureship at Harvard and "gives" material on the Civil War.

1960 *Apologies to the Iroquois* published.

1961 *Night Thoughts* published.

1962 *Patriotic Gore* published; travels to Canada to research Canadian literature.

1963 *The Cold War and the Income Tax* published; receives Presidential Medal of Freedom.

1964 Receives the Edward MacDowell Medal; works at the Center for Advanced Study, Wesleyan University.

1965 *O Canada* published.

1966   *The Bit between My Teeth* published; receives the Emerson-Thoreau medal and the National Medal for Literature.

1967   Returns to Israel in spring to update his Dead Sea Scrolls book.

1968   *The Fruits of the MLA* published in *The New York Review of Books.*

1969   Revision of Scrolls book, *The Dead Sea Scrolls,* published; the *Duke of Palermo and Other Plays* published.

1970   Suffers a slight stroke.

1971   *Upstate* published; works on Russian essays.

1972   Finds Naples, Florida, "boring"; another slight stroke in the spring; dies at the old stone house in Talcottville on June 12.

Introduction
Edmund Wilson: After 100

With Edmund Wilson's centenary year of 1995 behind us, there's a clear marker that has focused public attention on the career of a major American author. Wilson's work has been celebrated at the Mercantile Library in New York and at Princeton University, memorialized in the newspapers and journals, and reconsidered in a full-scale biography. Numbers of his essays have been printed in book form for the first time, and some of his books have been reprinted or are soon to reappear.[1] My 1985 book—essentially the story of Wilson's evolving talent—is reissued in the spirit of the centenary. The present introduction is meant to take note of several qualities of Wilson's mind that have become clearer to me in the last few years. My interests here concern Wilson's staying powers, his love of books, and his complex sense of himself.

Straightaway I would place Wilson in the first rank of twentieth-century essayists in English. He holds his place as one of those rare writers of nonfiction to whom other writers turn when they want to brace up their spirits and hear the sound of wonderfully constructed sentences on the march. Wilson has been film critic David Denby's "idol" and essayist Joseph Epstein's "literary equivalent" of Father Flanagan. He has had successors—prolific writers of solidly built essays—but none of them has been as comprehensive, as curious, as multifaceted, as philosophical and at the same time as grounded in the modern urban world. It's not that there are no contenders left on the field: George Steiner and Gore Vidal and Alfred Kazin—to name three very different figures— have covered the intellectual ground of the outreaching essayist, the erudite and eloquent writer who has a hold on many subjects and scorns the role of specialist. But these major figures—each superb in his own way—are not at home with Wilson's multitude of literary experiences and ideas and social actualities. Nor could they be. Wilson's confidence and directness in taking on his material have a nineteenth-century flavor. He learned to write before the First World War. In that unspecialized age, he developed an appetite for many varieties of knowledge, everything from the realms of speculative philosophy to the precincts of popular theater. His ease and curiosity were a feature of the progressive era, an eagerness to know many things and to alter the quality of life through that knowledge.

Did the great English essayists of the century—Woolf, Eliot, Leavis, Orwell—take on literature and society the way Wilson did? Orwell—at once the political barometer of his age and the lover of literature for its own sake—is the only genuinely comparable figure. F. R. Leavis was a powerful critic and moralist, but who would look to him as a gauge of the boom and bust years of the twenties and thirties? Who would look to Eliot's or Woolf's essays for a steady account of the unfolding of modernism and the impact of war and depression, class conflict and conformity? What writer of nonfiction could assume the role of guide through the traditions of the West, the undercurrents of minority culture, and the distracting, exhilarating social spectacle of 50 years? Wilson has been a luminous example of the man of letters, extraordinary because of the energy, the straightforwardness, and the concentrated purpose with which he fulfilled the promise of the role. He outwrote and outranged great American and English writers such as Lionel Trilling and Cyril Connolly. To locate the nearest essayist of his caliber in the Anglo-American world, we have to go back to George Santayana, the philosophical surveyor of literature, mind, and civilization.

"Alive, and everybody's business," Frank Kermode wrote of *Axel's Castle* in a 1961 piece. The comment—which I interpret in several ways—seems as accurate today as it was 35 years ago.[2] Sir Frank was writing about Wilson's ability to create excitement by poising himself between sympathy and judgment, attaching himself to literary works and then distancing himself from them as he analyzed, evaluated, and revealed the "master spirit" in the literature of an age. I would like to adapt and extend Kermode's argument by first showing how Wilson the literary critic remained true to his primary passion for literature—and yet faithful to his own skeptical nature. This blend of ardor and cool discipline—seeking new objects to love, qualifying and doubting his very passions—makes him a permanently useful critic, one who left a great deal of critical capital to be drawn on by people in our age of canon revision and multiculturalism. Thereafter I would like to say something about another aspect of Wilson's great talent, one that has become increasingly controversial in the past few years with the publication of his journals of the 1950s and 1960s—that of reporter on himself.

The stages of Wilson's progress as a writer reveal a classic kind of development, a return to the sources of his youthful inspiration: he began as a voracious reader and school-magazine critic of classics and new works; he went on to an early phase as reporter on and judge of the modernist movement and the modernity of the twenties; he devoted his middle years in large part to a romance with Marxism and historical criticism, although his ardors and admiration for socially aware writers never caused him to be fooled by agitprop; in the forties he resumed his boyhood enthusiasm for books as books, quite apart from their experimental or politically progressive qualities. Much as he had once loved and defended the new, he wasn't about to spend the rest of his life on it. He stayed with this last position until the end, mixing his own often idiosyncratic tastes in writing with a curious, cussed resistance to modern America. As he went his own way, he resisted categorization. With his surprising literary discoveries—books no one else would have lavished time on—his new angles on classics, his unpredictable forays into new books, and his championing of the unfashionable in what Irving Howe called the age of conformity, Wilson assumed the role of a Tory radical bookman, startling and troublesome to programmatic critics, and very much the independent, judgmental person he was when he set out as a young student.

Wilson was America's greatest defender of literature in the twentieth century—of the integrity of the artist, the dignity of the profession of letters, the worth of a well-written book. His passion for reading caused him to resist and combat the threats to good writing—even the noble ideas and ivory-towered isolations that stifled the vitality and honesty of a text. He was constantly drawing back from various outgrowths of literature, from cultural manifestations that seemed to many people to be a substitute for literature—ideologies, fads, popular sentiments, stereotypes, duplicable styles. These false equivalencies damaged the primary experience of something authentic. He struggled to overcome the conventions and attitudes that threatened to diminish art—whether the genteel constraints and heavily upholstered language of his youth, the radical slogans of his middle age, or the mass-culture tidal waves of his old age. In a review of Lionel Trilling's first book of criticism, he praised Matthew Arnold's sharp focus as a writer and contrasted it with Carlyle and Ruskin "drugging themselves with a rhetoric of the richest and most stultifying kind."[3] (Whether one agrees about Carlyle and Ruskin or not, the terms of his censure—overwriting and dullness—remain.) He directed similar attacks at the stiff-collar righteousness of the New Humanists—now a dimly remembered group of moral critics—and the all-purpose cant of the Communists. I can think of no instance in which

Wilson credits the postmodern world of TV, movies, and popular culture with nurturing the kind of talent he valued. The genteel, the politically driven, and the mass-directed would put no new or strangely antique charge on literature. He typically had to search the boulevards and byways of culture to find writers who would unsettle him and help him to challenge the average reader; he admired publishers who "took a chance on such outsize, outstyle or outsubject fiction" as Kate Chopin's *The Awakening* or James's "The Jolly Corner."[4]

A questioner of things established—academic opinions, middle-class tastes, women's secondary place in literary culture, literature as a high-class commodity—Wilson campaigned for change without using literary criticism as a form of political power. He welcomed the jolting effects of new works and developed an attitude—a pattern of judgment—that accommodated the unexpected and the original. But new works with their demands and their capacity to displace older tastes never caused Wilson to doubt the traditional dignity, continuity, and usefulness of the literary vocation. A writing life was not a mere field of influence, given shape and meaning by politics and social change. Instead it was an agreement of an individual in the present with those in ages past and future about the primary value of literature. A good writer was set apart from the other producers of cultural products, not because of the snob value of book writing as opposed to jingle writing or cartooning, but because of superior craftsmanship. And that craftsmanship—unlike most popular works—did not require the fuel of big money. In these convictions Wilson seems totally elitist to many contemporary writers and critics.

When working as a literary critic, Wilson set his terms and revealed the boundaries of his tolerance by refusing to get beyond the writer's vision to some theoretical conception of what literature should be. His cause was always books as opposed to abstractions and ideologies (he once wrote that Paul Elmer More could be trusted with ideas but not with literature). The writer as writer—not as moral reformer, not as activist, not as feminist, not as minority spokesman—was his primary object of attention. In the long run—after his disaffection with the left, his angry denunciation of our tax system in 1963, and his apologies to the Iroquois—he liked individual achievement better than social and political movements. (For that matter, his skepticism had been apparent in the age of commitment. Even in his 1930s mode in *To the Finland Station*—and certainly in his books of literary criticism and his collected chronicles such as *The Shores of Light* and *Classics and Commercials*—he treated ideas and causes less reverently than artistic selves: "isms" came and went and were no more sacrosanct than establishments.) The only thing that remained precious was the library, which had every species of literary practitioner. Wilson combined the author's insatiable curiosity with the nonprogrammatic radical's insistence on doing justice to the literary worker. His identification with George Saintsbury the connoisseur was mixed with his Marxist-Calvinist anger at the public and critics who could crush, mock, or ignore the good writer.

If a new generation were to study his offbeat judgments—his respect for Dawn Powell's "stout and self-sustaining" mind, his highlighting of the unromantic, "sardonic, steady, shrewd" humor of George Ade, his relentless search for the odd and the unacceptable in people and books, his admiration for the Zunis' fierce vitalism, and the impulse to get his own back in the early works of Kipling—its members would make the word *diversity* carry some weight.[5] For today's multiculturalists, diversity is a form of special-interest politics transplanted into the cultural realm; for Wilson the diversity among writers was a spectacle to be watched by critics and readers for curiosities, stylistic innovations, and energies. (He would certainly have agreed with Diana Trilling's view of multiculturalism—the Stalinism of its age, "moral virtue without reason.")[6] Many in our era think categories of writers are entitled to power; Wilson thought individual writers were entitled to a sympathetic hearing.

People of the 1990s could also stand to learn another Wilson lesson: true critical reformers do battle with conventions, not with continuities. Wilson's own career worked through many of the issues of today's canon debate; he was endlessly ingenious in keeping the lines open between innovation and tradition, a skill that few cultivate anymore. Even in *Axel's Castle,* published in 1930, what at first seemed like a wrenching break with the past—a symbolist aesthetic that "succeeded in throwing overboard completely the clarity and logic of the French classical tradition"—became a critic's occasion for finding connections, discovering that poetry is a continuous process and that the symbolists were "nourished from many alien sources." Even the wild men like Rimbaud and Verlaine who turned against the rational mind and distorted sense experience had their masters, and those masters in turn looked back to their own hermetic sources. Wilson found such forming and reforming of perceptions and representations exciting to observe. One of his basic—and best—stories as a reporter on literature was the unfolding of movements and tendencies and the ways writers remained unique yet part of a larger historical pattern.

And throughout his career Wilson was in search of the sometimes tangled filaments that connected unlikely writers of the past and off-center twentieth-century ones with contemporary readers. Why someone was "out"—and why he or she shouldn't be—was one of his favored kinds of argument: how to read Edna Millay out of season, how to reconnect with Dickens and Kipling at the tail end of the modernist movement, how to discover a part of your vital past that you never thought of. What do minor writers after the Civil War have to say to Americans in the age of the bomb? Wilson staged dramatic scenes in his essays to make his new readers part of little-known or misunderstood careers: Dickens in Warren's Blacking Factory is still news for students in undergraduate courses; many of Wilson's other essays are enriched by such defining scenes—the homosexual Henry Fuller looking at bustling Chicago social life, Marx writing while surrounded by children's playthings, Mallarmé at his Tuesdays, and Proust playing "host in the mansion where he is not long to be master." Wilson used these scenes to overcome the discontinuities of time, the gaps and breaks that might shut us off from writers who are good or great but many times outside our immediate range.

Although he never denied that his world was mired in disorder and was rapidly deconstructing itself through wars, new hatreds, and virulent ideologies, he insisted that literature could be a compensation for the whole mess. His 1920s essays in *The Shores of Light*—and several in *From the Uncollected Edmund Wilson*—are richly informed by his yearning for order and continuity: while society was anarchic, literature and criticism connected readers to a mastered world. Wilson did not share Ezra Pound's disgust with the spectacle of a run-down civilization, a heap of old books and broken statues. He wrote about supporting literary culture at the times when it was under threat—in the Gilded Age, in the midst of jazz-age commercialism, in the era of agitprop and 1940s Hollywood. These times, of course, were every time that touched his life—whether directly or through his immediate family history; it hardly need be said that Wilson conceived of the critic as a tireless combatant with whatever the politicians and their commercial cohorts dished up. In "The Anarchists of Taste: Who First Broke the Rules of Harmony, in the Modern World?" (1920), Wilson had his first real go at this problem of disordered modernity and the need for order. Twentieth-century literature can never feed off the harmonies of the eighteenth century. It's absurd to blame the artist, cry "literary Bolshevism," and label new work as anarchic nonsense.[7] Yet there is a high standard of craftsmanship, and Wilson gives a very understated description of it. The writer "can set down sharp little scenes with their appropriate emotions, in a style which, though conversational, achieves the definiteness of poetry." Sharpness and appropriateness: these two qualities seem to define the books Wilson praises throughout his career; they suggest the terms of what was never filled out as a personal canon. They also indicate that early in his career he had the fine critic's sense of what was well wrought and what was sloppy.

The sharp focusing of an image or an idea meant for Wilson the rejection of received wisdom, hearsay, groupthink, and other inferior forms of perception. Even flawed writers can succeed; his host of minor figures in *Classics and Commercials*—and even major figures that he doesn't especially like, such as Steinbeck—have a sharp eye and at their best a contempt for the predictable. But Wilson never allows them to coast. Saroyan is chided for lapsing into good-humored, mindless banter and for turning out the words and impressions like a columnist. Further down in the scale, Louis Bromfield and James M. Cain are two versions of what Hollywood could do to someone who thought of himself as a writer. In the first instance, it caused a novelist to forget that he was dealing in selves; his people seemed like mere billboard outlines. In the second instance, a writer with a gift for plot and on-the-edge drama lost himself in devils' parodies of slick scripts. Wilson uses the phrase "imitation book" in his essay "A Toast and a Tear for Dorothy Parker" (1944). By this he means the production that has no place beside that "rarity" in the 1940s—the real thing. High-handed and judgmental as this may sound to contemporary ears, it's a simple way of escaping all the recycled junk—from the conventional world of the past and from our trendy one—that we shouldn't be carrying into the future.

As for the real thing, Wilson felt it was often not in "the main stream." His view of literature, in Hubert Butler's incisive formulation, "had no piety, but much pietas"[8]—which is to say a vision of continuity that was no "orderly march-past of great writers." He had no qualms about putting a distance between himself and a big literary reputation: it's fascinating to observe him as the free-style judgmental critic, educating the reader in the ways of enthusiastic response and cool withdrawal. His 1958 essay " 'Miss Buttle' and 'Mr. Eliot' " in *The Bit between My Teeth* offers one of the best debunkings of old-fogyism and academic sterility available to us: it clearly demonstrates his ability to step back from the august culture of major writers and at the same time avoid losing his balance and becoming the trendy defender of inferior writers.

Some 20 years before critics started to decry elitism and hegemony, Wilson mounted a powerful and witty attack on "Main Line" literature: like the houses along suburban Philadelphia's best artery, it was a snobbish concept that excluded variousness and possibility. He added a good bit of bracing insult to his argument as he dismissed "the old-fashioned snobs and pedants like George Kittredge, Barrett Wendell and Irving Babbitt." And "Mr Eliot"—playing the role of Dr. Johnson "throning it in old London and laying down the rules of taste"—is (in various places in the essay) ridiculed for betraying the complexities of his own poetic vision. Just as T. S. Eliot lapses into the role of Mr. Eliot—the poet overwhelmed by the pontificator—so also does Samuel Johnson, the standard bearer and flexible critic of style, get lost in the posturing and pronouncements of Boswell's Johnson. This last harrumphing dictator is early identified in "Boswell and Others"—a 1925 piece in *From the Uncollected Edmund Wilson*—as a "man almost completely out of touch with the significant developments of his time." In "Reexamining Dr. Johnson," a 1944 essay from *Classics and Commercials,* the great critic is shown as having escaped from the smothering embraces of Boswell and the no less distorting and reductive accounts of modern academic biographers who often have a grudge against their subjects. Johnson's mind emerges as "far from . . . parochially local and hopelessly cramped by the taste of its age," as one that "saw literature in a long perspective and could respond to the humanity of Shakespeare as well as the wit of Pope." Between "Boswell and Others" and "Reexamining Dr. Johnson," Wilson had not changed a jot in his attitude toward the official academic world that worshipped Johnson, the stodgy character: the professors really liked rule making and pronouncing better than literary analysis and appreciation. At first this antiestablishment judgment sounds like a 1990s shot at elitist types in tweeds, but it goes far deeper than that.

It's true enough that Wilson—in famous essays like the "All-Star Literary Vaudeville" (1926 in *The Shores of Light)* and elsewhere—was opposed to those who were "content to close the canon," yet unlike most feminists and multiculturalists, Wilson was committed to a canon of literary selves, not to political positions or other locales where social ideals blossom. Writers were heterodox beings, their craft a law unto itself, their talents a matter of technical skill, emotional range, and imaginative and intellectual grasp, but not a question of political fervor. If he were alive in this age of culture wars, he would refuse the role of tradition's white knight: he always had a cool view of official spokesmen, especially if they sounded off about better times in the past and the dangers of contemporary experience. Wilson would also stand apart from multiculturalists and other fracturers of traditional standards of excellence; his position is clear enough in one of the most ambitious essays in *The Triple Thinkers,* "The Historical Interpretation of Literature." "Long-range" literature—the best kind—doesn't preach and doesn't necessarily seek any immediate social effects and doesn't quite know what it wants to say about the conditions of the moment.

After the Second World War, Wilson's reports on new writers became an occasional sideline: although his harvest of Kingsley Amis, Angus Wilson, and Saul Bellow is small, it reveals a great deal about how he used his convictions. His mind was flexible enough to find craft and durability in new places. Amis—for all his seediness and squalor—creates people who "have still something to build, to win." Angus Wilson—unlike many writers Wilson scored—is not a writer of "assimilable" satire (no mashed down prose, no "usual British product"); his work is "distinct from the well-bred and well-turned entertainment."⁹ Bellow explored one of Wilson's favorite topics in *Dangling Man,* the individual struggling for some autonomy against the backdrop of a "collective enterprise," in this case what Wilson considered America's immoral and unjust involvement in World War II.¹⁰ These newfound works were a part of a larger series of late discoveries. Wilson at age 50 was about to complete his career with a new kind of protest against the predictable. He wanted to prove that a radical bookman could dig deep into the reserves of his own spirit and find valuable goods—and these not writers or subjects that he had worked up for years. He took on writers and thinkers and even some activists—Ambrose Bierce with his dead-accurate prose style, Alexander Stephens with his exasperating integrity, Iroquois leaders with their immunity to stylishness, Russian stalwarts—that he had not said much or anything at all about. Wilson's mind retained its integrity, yet it worked in supple and surprising ways: Tolstoy is studied as a master of the aristocratic style, a prose that boldly risks clumsiness in the interests of precision; Turgenev is studied as a wounded artist who discovers the life-giving drop; and the newcomer Pasternak is discussed in terms of resurrection and the Russian Church. Style and transcendence, finding them left him almost no time for the new generation of countercultural and ethnic writers. In any case, Roth and Pynchon and Mailer were riding one of the highest publicity waves in literary history. They were well understood. Wilson's specialty had always been the misunderstood, the misheard, the out-of-step, the difficult, the seldom read. Who, after all, needed to be shepherded through

Goodbye, Columbus or *Advertisements for Myself?* The "out" figures—
Haitian poets of French extraction, Canadian writers, Jewish scholars
unknown to the general public, figures of culture in his father's frustrating Gilded Age—braced him up because they were more like himself.
No fabulous publicity machines were backing them up. He would be
their protector and revivifier, and along the way he would show his
enthusiasm for handmade styles and pugnacious messages. Wilson
staked his later career on this brave, unorthodox, and rather heedless
enterprise.

As we have come to learn more about Wilson the writer and man—
through the appearance of *The Fifties, The Sixties,* Jeffrey Meyers's 1995
biography, Rosalind Wilson's *Near the Magician,* and *From the Uncollected
Edmund Wilson*—it appears that he was a complex amalgam of firmness
and flexibility. He exerted authority in literary and cultural criticism
without laying down the law. Never was an American critic so at ease
with his standards, so possessed by his passions, and yet so nuanced in
his evaluations and undogmatic in his reactions. No wonder that he has
become less popular in America these past 20 years. In a country where
critics are known for their vehemence and the high concepts of their
books, Wilson's late works, especially, and the journals are coolly delib-
erative in their literary interpretations and remarkably free of theory and
doctrine. He rarely implied—the intemperate lapses about effete writers
in *A Piece of My Mind* are extraordinary exceptions—that the progress of
society was dependent on his views of literature. In the instance of late
collections—*The Bit between My Teeth, The Devils and Canon Barham, A
Window on Russia*—Wilson had no desire to argue his opinions to the
death or to end on a dramatic high note. What seems to have been at
work was his characteristic patient involvement with old loves and
curiosities, books and ideas that insulated him from a gigantic, menacing America. In writing about nineteenth-century books with their
leisurely (not to say interminable) prefaces, he put his situation this way
in *The Sixties:* "I find a certain solace in the murkiness and tangledness of
texts that leave so much of the past mysterious. They give me shelter
from the income tax problem, with which I must very soon deal."

In his last years he worked steadily to make sure that the narrative of
his own sensibility was completed: as writer and man, he asked only
that future readers know him as he was—which in fact was sometimes
not an attractive way to be. In his literary tastes, his social attitudes, and
his sexual exploits, he was sometimes hard to take. Why do we have to
be treated to his judgments of the Victorian author of *The Ingoldsby Leg-*

ends, Richard Barham—or for that matter to his thorough attempts to overcome our resistances to the dry novelist Maurice Baring? His forays into the neglected areas of literature and culture were not always appealing, and yet they never failed to reveal something curious or interesting about him. They expressed his love of "tangledness" and mysteriousness, his desire to confront what we would never have thought about. The essay about Canon Barham makes one of his characteristic brilliant connections: it shows the raucous and bizarre humor of a writer compensating for life in an age of epidemics, debtors' prisons, and staggering infant mortality rates. "One feels all through *The Ingoldsby Legends,* for all the rattling jollity of the verse, an uneasiness of danger and pain." Ultimately we are not bored by Baring simply because we are imbibing Wilson's steady, clear, and informative reactions to yet another flawed writer with a gift for social observation.

Wilson's evaluations of people and the state of our nation are also always reflections of his true nature; they never seem to be posturings or ill-considered comments, and yet, it must be conceded that he sometimes bullied his way through personal relations and large issues. In *The Sixties* many of his casual comments on his children and old friends are, to say the least, an embarrassment. Like Mr. Punch (who was the central figure in the puppet shows he staged for his family in his later years), he relished the exhilarating exercise of his own destructive powers. Wilson-Punch could finish off his wife and family and exult in his freedom. He could damage people's dignity and crow about it. All, of course, in the spirit of criticism, a passion that included some very blunt self-criticism. In one journal entry, the fat, red-faced old drinker looks at himself in the mirror and contrasts his reflection with that of his lovely wife; the fogy of *Upstate* doesn't mind sinking deeper into his own narrowed perceptions. Perhaps this is the trouble: Wilson rather enjoyed his own faults and limitations. The heedless part of his nature was not confined to the private realm—anyone who has read *The Cold War and the Income Tax* knows how off-the-pier Wilson can be about the function of government and the uses of taxation. (Isaiah Berlin has remarked that when Wilson missed his target, he missed it by many miles.)[11] He does not seem to mind appearing like an ignorant adolescent or irascible cane brandisher as he critiques big government. For a writer who had reported on public affairs in the *New Republic*—who subtly analyzed the New Deal and had such insight into the state of the nation in the 1930s—Wilson seems to have become strangely and belligerently unaware of what his tax dollars were going for: defense spending and

other shameful adventures were hardly the whole picture of America in
the years after World War II. That "son of a bitch Uncle Sam" also does
not sound as good to 1990s ears as it did in the early 1960s: it's arresting and funny, but rather simplistic and scary.[13]

The sexual material in the journals of the fifties and sixties—no news
to those who have followed the earlier solidly packed, graphic install-
ments—became curiously creepy as the aging performer-connoisseur-
chronicler turned to writing about several young friends—not to mention his own wife. We sense something mortifyingly intimate and
unnecessary, and at first we sympathize with Joseph Epstein's observation: Why is this material in print? But no sooner do we draw away from
Wilson's candid, crude revelations than we are forced to consider why
any unattractive aspect of a writer's writing career should be brought
forward. Why is it necessary to know about Joyce's scatological letters
to Nora? Why is it necessary to know about Wilson's descriptions of his
Upstate girlfriends? To my mind the answer isn't at all complicated:
because the material is there and because it will allow people in other
times to see how a writer felt and expressed himself about private
things. These things have a bearing on a writer's vision of human
motives and value. (And they are not, I should add, dug-up dirt and
hearsay; they are part of the writer's life work.) In Wilson's case, the
answer is also that he wanted to give a detailed account of what he was
in youth, maturity, and old age. And once said, we must remember the
style of his revelations. The old passion-distance asserts itself on almost
every page of the journals: desire recollected in tranquillity, if you will,
but not mere lust. Yes, it's a bit macabre to listen to a great man of letters retailing impressions of his wife's body, but what redeems Wilson's
anatomical accounting is a seriousness about sex and love that sets him
apart from sensationalists. This quality made the once shocking "The
Princess with the Golden Hair" so much more than a titillating account
of an intellectual's affairs with a proletarian and a princess.

The moment Wilson begins to write about sex—whether he's coarse
or delicate—he's the critic evaluating the interplay of mind and body.
Looking at himself, he wonders about the nature of desire, the spectacle
of his own aging body, the waning of his own impulses, the meaning of
his encounters. He stands off from the scenes of his own passion, reporting calmly. In one episode recounted in *The Fifties,* he captures himself in
all his subtlety and ambiguity: enjoying lovemaking al fresco with his
wife Elena at Duck Pond in Wellfleet, but more intensely enjoying the
sight of his beloved later on, at a distance. "Afterwards, I walked around

the pond, feeling perfectly happy—enjoyed the sight of a painted turtle swimming from the shore to the depths. I looked back at Elena from time to time—she was taking a nap: I loved to see her—her bare legs and blue clothes (skirt and sweater)—and know that she was still with me, and that we could still be happy together in the open air on the beach." There's nothing of the pornographer's crude energy as Wilson leads us away from the scene, into his meditative world. Like Montaigne he wants to philosophize about his animal-spiritual nature, watch it heat up and cool off. Wilson in his journals of the fifties and sixties echoes the attitudes and moods of Montaigne's "On Some Lines from Virgil." In taking stock of his passions, Montaigne is at once austere and pleasure-loving—the philosopher who fears the "insensible" state of old age and wants to "deliberately let myself go a bit to license."[13] Wisdom "has its excesses" for Montaigne and "for fear I may dry up, wither, and grow heavy with prudence . . . I amuse myself in the remembrance of my past youth." Wilson, who had no spent youth at Princeton to look back on, amuses himself by recounting small and large escapades from the phases of adult life—in one breath calling himself silly, in the next tracking his own often pathetic limitations. Like Montaigne's explorations, the passages in Wilson are a deliberate exercise in imprudence; they defy age and convention. The French essayist's curiosity and control are very close to Wilson's way of presenting his inner nature: especially in his later years Wilson wanted to inspect his being and make a report on it for posterity; yet he wanted to be the artist and the doubter as well, the creator of himself who didn't leave a mere confession. There is always the insistence upon veracity and precision—including that turtle and the blue clothes—always the skill to make those facts about his nature and surroundings resonate with tension, irony, and skepticism. The tender sex scene ends with this: "When I got home, I drank some whisky and was out like a light before six—put myself to bed above my study and didn't come to till three in the morning, when I had an awful dream that Elena was dead and went over to the other side of the house to find her. My sexual powers must be definitely flagging. I was sixty ten days ago." Wilson's journals will probably stand as one of the most ambitious attempts of an American in the twentieth century to record the actualities of mind and body: on every page he can report on his own fluctuating being while seeing it against the backdrop of history and what an eighteenth-century writer would call general human nature.

Edmund Wilson Revisited tries to clear up the errors of my 1985 text—gaffes and oversights that would have irritated Wilson no end. (The secondary sources have been brought up to date with a generous selection of reviews, essays, recollections of the author, and larger studies.) Despite Wilson's personal lapses in taste and sense, his achievement continues to inspire as it intimidates. He has been one of my models since I discovered his work in the late 1960s. I hope that my account of his intellectual and personal life will attract new readers to his work. The tension and poise, passion and discipline of his prose are permanently important for American civilization.

Chapter One
The Progress of a Mind

Edmund Wilson's work provides an exception to Alexis de Tocqueville's prophetic remarks about the direction of literature in a democracy. In the 1840s the French sociologist predicted that American writers would be "fantastic, incorrect, overburdened, and loose" in style, that they would aim at imaginative effects rather than profundity of thought and erudition. The solidity and classicism of Wilson's style, his balance and clarity, and his earnest dialogue with his time and with other cultures set him apart from the wild and often provincial strain in American literature. He is our enlightenment figure, a *philosophe* in an age of world wars, depressions and class conflicts, rising taxes, lowering standards, intellectual bewilderment, bombs, revolutions, and bureaucracies. While our greatest writers from Poe to Faulkner and Mailer have immersed themselves in the destructive element—and have created bizarre styles to represent the fragmented and convulsed America they gave themselves to—Wilson cultivated the aesthetics of plain communication: in the manner of an eighteenth-century man of letters, he believed that words could right wrongs, unconfuse issues, and unclog the minds of his fellow citizens. He lived and worked to further the cause of rational inquiry and scorned mystics, doomsayers, and others who claimed to commune with darkness and light. He took possibility, not ecstatic transcendence, as his territory. His characteristic literary form, the extended essay, reflects his rationalist commitment to limited exploration and personal judgment; it also reveals a kind of artistic bravery and individuality in a country gone mad in pursuit of the Great American Novel and other spectacular performances.

For the better part of our century, Wilson practiced the writer's profession with an astonishing steadiness of purpose and diversity of activity. He wanted his readers to understand modern art, politics, and culture, and he assumed various roles to show them what he had discovered about the texture of life and the tendencies of ideas and books since the French Revolution. Basically a journalist, he took the nineteenth and twentieth centuries as his beat. In order to do his reporting fully and accurately, he became a social critic, literary critic, observer of pop culture and the lively arts, historian, travel writer, linguist, poet, play-wright, and novelist. He managed to fall in love with each role without losing his sense of unity. His way of being a professional seems diffuse and difficult in our age of specialization. Without establishing a resting place for his talents—without committing himself to a fixed professional function—he became a figure whose authority and insight are national resources. A professor without a university, a critic without a field, a historian without a period, he became the exemplary intellectual of his generation. He left a wheelbarrow full of books on subjects diverse enough to challenge the ambitions of a Renaissance humanist, and he supplied American literature with a talent unique in range, intelligence, and lucidity.

Born in 1895 in Red Bank, New Jersey, Wilson became part of a family that was rich in traditions and achievements. The Wilsons and the mother's family, the Kimballs, were typical of the dignified and public-spirited professional people of the late nineteenth century. Edmund Wilson Sr. was a Princeton man, a prominent attorney, and a notable figure in state politics. The son of a Presbyterian minister, he was nurtured on the work ethic and the ideal of dedication to a mission. Edmund Jr. took pride in writing about the way his father cleaned up the rackets in Atlantic City, worked for low fees, and almost made it to the Supreme Court under Woodrow Wilson's administration. In the Gilded Age—the era of railroad moguls, overstuffed furniture, and con-spicuous consumption—the father maintained his integrity at the expense of the pleasure principle. A staunch Republican, and dinner-table tyrant, the elder Wilson bequeathed a legacy of Calvinism to his son. Edmund Jr. was to become the author of upwards of 30 books. Like the great Victorians Carlyle and Ruskin, he worked prodigiously and, whether he knew it or not, lived up to his Puritan forebears' standards by spurning frivolity and proving his specialness with book after book.

He began writing in the nursery. His first book, a collaboration with his cousin Sandy, was stitched into a volume by a literary aunt. Throughout childhood he produced a stream of stories and sketches, diaries and poems. At 60 he reflected on the way his style was formed: his father, it seems, left more than the legacy of hard work. In an age of fancy oratory and windy prose, the elder Wilson cultivated the plain style—the verbal manner of Lincoln. Wilson came to feel that "this model was a valuable heritage, like the table pieces of silver of the Paul Revere silversmith period which have come down to me from his side of the family."

In addition to this model of clarity, Wilson's father provided material enough for rebellion. The father's disciplined life was punctuated by a number of serious nervous breakdowns, caused in no small way by his rigidity, his driven and bleak attitude. Wilson himself was later constantly at odds with his father's preachments, fixed views on politics and society, and self-righteousness. The Wilson home was a dispiriting place to be young in, and Edmund sought the easiest avenue of escape—his mother's family. The Kimballs, also established in New Jersey, owned an old stone house in Talcottville, New York. They were originally New Englanders—Wilson was related to Cotton Mather—who had migrated to New York State at the end of the eighteenth century. It was at Talcottville that Wilson first experienced the romance and beauty of rural life. He spent his boyhood summers in the old house and claimed that it was the place where he first discovered his literary vocation. In the heart of old, almost exotically primitive America, the little boy felt he was a poet. "No," he said after reconsidering, "I am not quite a poet, but I am something of the kind." Talcottville, as symbol and reality, fed his imagination until the end of his life. It contained a whole constellation of ideas and feelings: the spirit of independence and freedom, continuity with the past, escape from conventions, the sense of baronial superiority and dignity. This pocket of the past was both a retreat and a center of his values.

His boyhood years were dominated by other influences as well. Wilson, the keeper of notebooks, made the recording of his life part of his art.[1] The young boy also spent a good deal of time at the Kimballs' home in Laurelwood, New Jersey. The grandparents and uncles there were worldlier than the Wilsons and lived on the fringes of great wealth. Wilson enjoyed gardening and playing as well as being introduced to the Greek classics by his uncle. It was almost paradisiacal after the time spent with the puritanical Wilsons. Here, too, there was something to rebel against. The neighboring "Finches"—actually the Jay Goulds— had a little boy with whom Wilson was brought to play. Their display of the brute power of money struck Wilson with a shock that lasted a lifetime.[2] The rich boy lived in ducal splendor and was as imperious as a grand seigneur; the young Wilson was struck by the injustice of such an overlord class, and his visits to the Gould home were like so many bad dreams about American life.

Soon after this period Wilson was enrolled at Hill School in Pottstown, Pennsylvania. His mother escorted him there and caused him considerable embarrassment by using his nickname, Bunny, derived not from "rabbit" but from "plum bun." The name stuck and appears throughout Wilson's life on his letters. The young boy began his career in one of the country's most demanding and austere schools; the place, as described in *The Triple Thinkers,* was the perfect complement to the elder Wilson's attitudes:

> the remorseless paternalism of the Hill had something of the suffocating repressive effect of the Pennsylvania mill-town in which the company owns the workers' houses, controls their contacts with the outside world, and runs the banks, the schools, and the stores.

The school monitored its students' inner lives as well; the Calvinist doctrine of sin and regeneration was the principle that organized school life, and itinerant preachers came from New York to promulgate what Wilson described as a "lachrymose and mealy-mouthed virility." Wilson treated the oily excesses of all this in "Galahad," a beautifully told initiation story. At Hill, religious fervor was at such a pitch that the headmaster's wife used to oversee the boys' spiritual lives by questioning them in private interviews. Wilson—the literary, aloof adolescent—was reminded of the "temptation" of "neglecting his relations with his fellows."

But at Hill he also met John Rolfe, a teacher of Greek, who offered balance to the sloppy evangelicalism by providing a model of humanistic dedication, intellectual rigor, and individualism. Wilson was fascinated by the man's sophistication, his tough comic sense, and his devotion to classical ideals of rectitude and excellence that antedated Christianity. The boy immersed himself in the Greek classics, wrote essays for the Hill School *Record,* and went through a decisive religious unconversion. Like a number of Victorian sages, Wilson was able to pinpoint the exact time when he stopped believing in the efficacy of organized religion. A sentence from the preface to Shaw's *Major Barbara* precipitated his lifelong unbelief: "At present there is not a single credible established religion in the world." Wilson eventually dispersed this sentiment throughout his works; its full meaning came to include a distrust of ideologies and establishments of any sort.

Even before Wilson arrived at Princeton in 1912, he was filled with the excitement of reading great literature and the thrill of trying his own hand at writing. At Hill he had exacting training in grammar and rhetoric under an Englishman, Dr. John A. Lester. He absorbed the idea that a piece of writing should honor a trinity of values: "Lucidity, Force, Ease." And with this rather old-fashioned sentiment in mind, he proceeded to set up as a teenage literary critic. He not only produced numerous essays for the *Record* but also began writing letters in which he handed out judgments and advice to friends. He became a kind of literary father confessor, steering his friends away from trashy books, evaluating their prose styles, and offering them an astonishing range of instructive comparisons of books.[3]

At Princeton his enthusiasm for literature was fed by brilliant classmates and extraordinary teachers, but his contempt for leisure and conspicuous consumption—acquired at his grandparents' home in Laurelwood—was further aroused. The university's atmosphere, he recalls, was hardly conducive to the development of his own ideals. Princeton men of the period, busy with their eating clubs—"monuments to the mediocrity of human taste and ideals," according to Wilson—were not about to espouse anything smacking of ungentlemanly rigor and ambition. "Yale," Wilson remarks, "was a burning religion, with, however, a good many unbelievers; Princeton, a well-dressed and convivial group, to which, if one were not convivial, it was easy to remain indifferent." Throughout his life Wilson distrusted the Princeton ethos and loved to quote his third wife, Mary McCarthy, who felt that Princeton failed to give its men the discipline necessary to be writers.

Wilson was not, in the words of his professor Christian Gauss, "in the least rah-rah or collegiate" and couldn't endure editorials in the campus paper about "The High Cost of Dancing."[4] He found friends on *The Nassau Lit* and in humanities preceptorials. There was the distinguished poet John Peale Bishop, a self-possessed young craftsman and something of an aesthete; Stanley Dell, a friend from Hill and Princeton class poet; T. K. (Teek) Whipple, the editor of the *Lit,* who asked Wilson to join the magazine as a freshman.[5] Another friend was F. Scott Fitzgerald, the enfant terrible of the group, the one who didn't study and couldn't spell but who would celebrate Princeton in *This Side of Paradise.* These men were the inner core; not destined to sell bonds after graduation, they pursued literature with passion and intensity.

Wilson was the most serious and scholarly, although Phi Beta Kappa was not interested in him because he earned poor grades in math and science.[6] He did a phenomenal amount of reading in literature and philosophy, continued his classical studies, and worked under the great humanist Christian Gauss.[7] One of the finest teachers of the twentieth century, Gauss was, in H. L. Mencken's words, "everything a college professor never is." Neither a fuddy-duddy textual scholar nor a philosophizing gasbag, Gauss was the scholar as man of the world. Wilson was

always impressed by the fact that his teacher had been a journalist in
Paris, had known Oscar Wilde, and, some said, had let his hair grow
down to his shoulders and tried all the drugs mentioned in Baudelaire.
The strong bohemian-aesthete strain captured the imagination of the
young escapee from Calvinism. Gauss's "field" was European literature,
but he gave Wilson something much larger. If Wilson's father had
bequeathed to him a sense of mission, and if Rolfe had offered him classical polish, Gauss offered his "unusual fluidity of mind," his ability to
move easily among ideas and historical settings. Gauss was the kind of
teacher "who starts trains of thought that he himself does not guide to
conclusions." The trains of thought he set up in Wilson were aesthetic
and moral. Through his teaching he dealt with "the artist's morality as
something that expressed itself in different terms than the churchgoer's
or citizen's morality; the fidelity to a kind of truth that is rendered by
the discipline of aesthetic form."

Such ideas were not completely new to Wilson, but Gauss's subtlety
made them a permanent feature of his intellectual life. Gauss once asked
his student, "Where do you think our ideals come from—justice, righteousness, beauty, and so on?" Wilson answered, "Out of the imagina-
tions of men." "That is correct," the teacher replied. This lesson of the
master—that imagination, not institutions and codes and mass movements, creates our world of values—was one that Wilson would use to
inform his political masterpiece, *To the Finland Station*.

When Wilson graduated from Princeton in 1916, he was rich in such
ideas, experienced as a literary man, but quite untouched by ordinary
life. Despite his disdain for snobs and idlers, he was "entirely unable to
get on with ordinary people." He was also "too shy with proper young
girls who were only just learning to be improper." His classmates had
voted him most likely bachelor, and he, too, considered himself unsuited
to conventional marriage. In the summer of that year, without any particular patriotic sense, he went up to Plattsburgh, New York, and
enlisted in a military preparedness unit. He couldn't learn to shoot a
rifle and was bored by the whole episode. Back in New York City he
worked for a short time as a reporter for the *Evening Sun* but lacked the
push to get a good story. Soon after that he enlisted in an army hospital
unit—an alternative to being drafted.

When he got "over there," he felt the way many disaffected Americans did: the horror of "blowing people to shreds whom you had never
seen" weighed on him. Although, like Hemingway, he worked among
the wounded, he had an acute sense of guilt and hopelessness. The feel-

ing is recorded in "The Death of a Soldier," a story later published in a cynical collaboration called *The Undertaker's Garland*. Wilson austerely narrates the journey of a young man who is shifted across Western Europe and dies of pneumonia. The senselessness of suffering is presented in the spare style and with the restraint and tense understatement that we have come to associate with Hemingway. Wilson's young victim's pockets are emptied after death—and the contents are enumerated with a matter-of-factness that generates a quiet despair. Wilson, like Hemingway, is no patriot and establishes a separate peace with his fellow soldiers. In another story, "Lieutenant Franklin," Wilson goes a step further and expresses a man's fellow feeling for all the people caught up in the war; by fraternizing with the conquered Germans, the young officer runs afoul of the army.

In *A Prelude* (1967), his first volume of notebooks, Wilson sums up the impact of the war: "I indicted the institutions of the Western World and suggested a way out in the direction of socialism." Socialism was a humane impulse rather than a set of precepts; it was something that the young writer connected with a new awareness of ordinary people. Wilson saw a moral and social opportunity and underwent another great change: "It suddenly became very clear to me that I could never go back to my former life—that is, that I could never go back to the habits and standards of even the most cultivated elements of the world in which I had lived." That world was destroyed by the "liberating effect" of his experience with the army, his new associations and new feelings.

Beginning in the twenties, Wilson's notebooks swell to Tolstoyan proportions; often rather repetitive, they nevertheless present a brilliant pageant of his ideas and artistic experiments as well as a cavalcade of political and social life in the age of the flapper. Living and working became exceedingly complex for Wilson as he divided his attention and energy among magazine positions, writing projects, and an exhausting number of friendships and erotic relationships. He began the twenties with a burst of energy and ended them with a nervous breakdown. He started working as a freelance writer after the war, and by 1920 he was on the staff of *Vanity Fair*. A year later he was managing editor of the *New Republic;* the position offered more opportunity to write and a more serious forum for his ideas than did the rather slick *Vanity Fair*. At the *New Republic* Wilson found a place to publish, although he didn't keep the editorship for long. During the decade and well into the thirties, he produced an astonishing amount of topical journalism, stories that ranged from "The Follies as an Institution" to ironic reflections on the

Sacco and Vanzetti trial. He did theater reviews in 1923 for *The Dial*, and during the same period he reviewed large numbers of books and wrote longer analytic essays on Fitzgerald, Pound, Joyce, and other writers of the age. All this he accomplished as he pursued his own work, that is, the larger creative and critical undertakings. *The Crime in the Whistler Room*, a play about the challenge to the repressive social forces in America, was produced in 1924—its central female character was played by Wilson's new wife, Mary Blair. *Discordant Encounters*, a series of dialogues about social and cultural problems, appeared in 1926. By 1928 he had conceived and started work on *Axel's Castle*, his pioneering exploration of the modern experimental tradition in literature. By 1929 he had finished his novel *I Thought of Daisy*—his attempt to capture the temper of the twenties as well as to find a durable and coherent self.

Life itself was rather incoherent for Wilson before the market crash. By the time he landed in the Clifton Springs Sanitarium in March 1929, his marriage to Mary Blair was over. He was the father of a daughter, Rosalind. He had also become a prodigious womanizer. Early in the decade he had met and fallen in love with America's greatest woman poet, Edna St. Vincent Millay. She went to Paris, however, and the luckless Wilson never really caught up with her, except as an ideal in *I Thought of Daisy*. He turned to a number of affairs, which are, as Leon Edel has noted, documented with zoological precision in his notebooks.[8] There was Anna, a Ukrainian waitress and dance-hall girl, who is a major character in Wilson's journals—and a life-availing symbol in his later novel *Memoirs of Hecate County*. There were also a few nameless bodies with whom Wilson records his transactions. And there was Margaret Canby, a well-born and genial California woman, who was his drinking companion and, by 1930, his new wife.

Socially, there were the sensations of the twenties: Dorothy Parker at *Vanity Fair*, reeking of perfume and crackling with wit; Scott and Zelda Fitzgerald, raising a ruckus on two continents; parties broken up by the cops. While Wilson lovingly and meticulously recorded it all, he also took its measure; although he was part of the chaos, as a writer and spectator he wanted to shape meanings and designs that his contemporaries were frequently too involved and too passionate to care about. As the most contemplative and learned man around—one whose mind sought generalizations about the Jazz Age while Fitzgerald and Dos Passos were involved with its tempo—Wilson formulated an aesthetic: literature was a result of our "rude collisions" with reality; out of these "shocks" the artist can create "an orderly pattern." Wilson, the man of reason, writes of the "logic of our reason and the harmony of our imagination" that generate a literary work. In his own not-so-harmonious life, he felt that his writing was a "compensation for the disappointments and humiliations of a life which never hit the mark or suited the means to the end."

As the thirties opened, Wilson was exhilarated while bankers and brokers were "taking a beating." There was some hope for renewal in the spectacle of economic collapse. In the twenties he had worked on a novel and a critical book that looked to art as a principle of coherence; he would now consider social solutions and revolution as ways of reshaping life. The fact of the Great Depression caused him to bring into focus ideas and emotions about community and social reform that he had been dealing with haphazardly since the war. He at first became the recording secretary of American misery, then the observer of the Soviet experiment, and finally the Balzacian chronicler of nineteenth- and twentieth-century socialists and radicals. His intellectual stance during the thirties was at once representative of his generation and highly individual. To be sure, he was the leftist intellectual disillusioned with boom-bust economics and the Anglo-Saxon man of letters in revolt against his own background. He was also the critic defending art against the inroads of propaganda and the ambivalent historian of radicalism who had a dream of autonomy that transcended movements, doctrines, and meetings.

As a journalistic witness to the American jitters (for the *New Republic,* principally), he traveled around the country during the depression and reported on the panorama of suffering: from "Mr. and Mrs. X," the educated and genteel victims, the managerial people who stood to lose everything, to the striking miners of Pineville, Kentucky, to the families living on three dollars a week and eating corn mixture meant for cows. *The American Earthquake* and his notebooks, *The Thirties,* are reports submitted on the magnitude of spiritual and economic depression. Both books are filled with carefully researched and observed accounts of strikers, the unemployed, and the destitute. Taken in conjunction, they constitute the emotional, social, and political material of an epic. Wilson was not content to produce descriptions of a string of debacles commented on by a sensitive spectator, however. He wanted to create a grand drama of class conflict and ideology. By this time in his career, he suspected that he wasn't really a novelist at heart; the materials he had collected about politics and society suggested, as usual with Wilson, broad generalizations. He began preparing himself to write his own kind of epic, a historical retelling of nineteenth- and twentieth-century socialism, encrusted with personalities and brimming with consequences. What was before him in America—the bread lines and the civil unrest—was a spectacle informed by a hundred years of strife. He would trace the ideas that had led Lenin to the Finland Station and that were now leading America leftward. Meanwhile, Wilson put himself on the line politically: he stood at the barricades with the strikers in Pineville and got run out of town by the police. Disgusted with Hoover's inertia and Roosevelt's "Boy Scout" smile, he voted Communist in 1932. He became so caught up in political and social turmoil that his dream life became part of the drama: "I dreamed I was a chapter of a Malraux novel—I was riot with lots of fighting and violence." In another dream he was being attacked by the American Legion—a prophetic dream in light of what happened to him in the 1950s.

His anxieties were also personal. Margaret Canby had died in an accident in 1932. Their marriage had been boozy and troubled, but his journals record considerable tenderness. He loved Margaret, but his aloof nature—the very quality that allowed him to sympathize with artists who watched life rather than lived it—made him a hard man to live with. She referred to him as "Old Man Gloom Himself" and also as "a cold fishy leprous person." Wilson was acutely aware of this aloof side of his nature. Living in New York, he sensed "the arid logical emotional vacuum in which I found I had landed myself." He wanted to make contact with people, and yet the castle of art, ideas, and impersonal work was where he dwelt most of the time.

He was drawn to the warmth, sexuality, and kindness of Anna; he fantasized about living with her in Brooklyn and saying good-bye to the literary pretenses of Manhattan. Yet always the desire asserted itself "to be quite by myself, sufficient to myself and not responsible to anybody." The conflict between these two desires foreshadows the dynamic tension of the rest of his career: he was to spend his life shuttling between castles and human contacts, between abstractions and concrete experiences. Out of this tension he would create two kinds of art: he would clarify the work of great artists and thinkers, and conversely, he would generalize and abstract large themes from the welter of experience. The two sides of Wilson remind us of the two kinds of poets described by Coleridge: one poet makes the exotic clear and familiar to the reader; the other makes the familiar more than it at first appears.

Wilson the clarifier went to the Soviet Union on a Guggenheim Fellowship in 1935. Already having germinated the idea for *To the Finland*

Station, he wanted to examine the texture of a revolutionary society and to find the reality behind the bugaboo of communism. He studied Russian with a tutor, went to ballets and museums, visited manufacturing plants and cooperative farms, and spent some time in a rural hospital recovering from scarlet fever. He was impressed by people who were getting things done without class distinctions; the experience also reinforced his belief that people under socialism were not automata. He tried to replace the "big scare" approach to the Soviets with a sober and humanistically critical view of an evolving society. And, as always, in evaluating power he was distrustful in his responses. Although he didn't roundly condemn the Stalin cult, he identified the characteristic amnesia about the tyranny of recent history and was quite blunt about his own communist "convictions": he admitted that he would not "last a half hour" as a communist.

As the decade drew to a close, Wilson published *The Triple Thinkers,* another work of clarification in which he enlightens Americans about neglected writers and muddled subjects. The book's showpiece is a nuanced dialectical essay on Marxism and literature—an attempt to distinguish between "long range" artists and "short range" propagandists. Such work became a part of the rational bulwark that Wilson built for his readers, but it did little for him financially. These were lean years for a writer living off magazine writing. His marriage to Mary McCarthy in 1938—described by him indirectly as "hideous" and directly as "nightmarish"—brought new responsibilities and a son, Reuel Kimball. Wilson needed money, and the offer of a $1,200 teaching position at the University of Chicago seemed attractive. He gave his students a chapter in his new project, *The Wound and the Bow.* This book is in many ways a landmark synthesis. In it Wilson combines the sociopolitical and psychological-aesthetic strains in his writing; he also casts new light on very familiar literary figures like Dickens and Kipling while at the same time considering how these standard authors have been buried under an avalanche of conventional responses. He shows how the imprint of personal and social suffering plays a role in an artist's career; part Freudian, part Marxist, Wilson is wholly sensitive to art itself. Without slinging jargon, he became America's preeminent practitioner of psychological criticism.

The war years were another period of literary simultaneity. Wilson had by now opened up new fronts in his career—most notably the psychological—and he was ready to combine new insights in another novel about American society, *Memoirs of Hecate County.* This creepy Gothic allegory of American failure is ostensibly about suburban sex and the situation of intellectuals. Superficially, it reads like a series of stories, but it affects the reader in powerful ways. For a time the courts banned the book, and Wilson became a celebrity. Harry Truman's White House ordered a copy; the young John Updike borrowed it from a Pennsylvania library. Wilson, almost without knowing it, had invented an authentic American art form—the suburban shocker.

During the war Wilson lived at some distance from many of his fellow intellectuals. While most of them joined in the fight against fascism, Wilson assumed an isolationist position and made no bones about his disdain for the war effort. Alfred Kazin reports that Wilson "saw Pearl Harbor as a plot for Roosevelt." He severed his connection with the *New Republic* in 1941 and intellectually sat out the war years while others were fervid. While his "political acuteness" seemed more than questionable to Kazin and other writers and thinkers, his "flinty old American trust in his own opinions was his flair, his style, his enormous charm"; this remained as an example of personal fortitude, if not proper response.

The forties were also a period of intense critical activity for Wilson: *The Boys in the Back Room,* an account of what California had done to writers, came out; he reviewed widely for *The New Yorker;* he reflected on the American scene as he wrote of Fitzgerald's death; he became an anthologist in *The Shock of Recognition.* He traveled to Europe at the end of the war and was revolted by the decadence and disorder of the civilization that had produced Proust and Joyce. Just as his reporting of the depression in the early thirties had prepared him for the intellectual blockbuster *To the Finland Station,* this period was a staging area for a series of mammoth explorations. His discontent was again about to erupt into wide-ranging studies.

Meanwhile, during the forties Wilson developed a strong friendship with Vladimir Nabokov, the Russian émigré and man of letters whose novel *Lolita* would explode onto the American scene in 1957. Wilson helped Nabokov deal with publishers and gave him advice about academic positions; Nabokov offered Wilson literary advice and also provided him with a private window on Russia and the world of the intelligentsia. In a correspondence that spanned more than 30 years, the two writers engaged in one of the more remarkable jousting matches in recent American letters—a genial, but often ironic quarrel about Marxism and the left, literary style, Russian versus English versification, and contemporary writers. Together in print in *The Nabokov-Wilson Letters,* they seem like two brilliant vaudevillians firing elegantly turned quips and performing their special routines: Wilson, the author of a book that praised Lenin, the intense inquirer into the social and political problems of the age; Nabokov, the suave and playful man of the world who dismisses radical dreams of a better socialist world and is totally literary. "Volodya" liked *To the Finland Station,* despite the "little thistles of conventional radicalism sticking to your freely flowing gown." He corrected Wilson's celestial colors in the portrait of Lenin's father. In turn Wilson, the neoclassical stylist, did the rationalist's job of criticizing Nabokov's puns and bizarre flights; he found the situation in *Lolita* (pedophilia) "repulsive," the plot "absurd," and the whole work "hazy" and unclear in design. But Wilson's negative response to his friend's work about love and sex might have been a response to a 1946 letter that Nabokov wrote about Wilson's own sexually controversial *Memoirs of Hecate County.* The book, Nabokov wrote, was "as pure as a block of ice in a surgical laboratory." The two writers exchanged such insights until Wilson's death.

A less durable relationship, Wilson's marriage to Mary McCarthy, ended in 1946 and was soon followed by another. After the rivalry and stimulation of living with one of America's most incisive women—a critic and fiction writer who was cultivating some of the same political and social acreage as Wilson—life with Elena Mumm Thornton, an elegant European who was a member of the Champagne family, was less hectic. The relative harmony of their marriage provided the right atmosphere for a writer who was about to submit himself to Herculean tasks of research and writing.

When Wilson returned from postwar Europe, he saw an America that was suffering from a not-so-new spiritual ailment. The complacency and repression that had so affected his father's generation was again in the ascendant: the victors had come home to be pleased with themselves and to make war on dissidents, libertarians, and naysayers. Wilson dramatized the disease in his 1951 play *The Little Blue Light,* a work that inaugurates a new phase of his attack on American life. Bread lines and strikers were no longer the problem. Below the increasingly sleek surface of society there were "thought police," organized criminals, and manipulators of consciousness. While the hardships of the thirties were bracing to a man disillusioned with capitalism, the insidiousness of the fifties was a genuine cause for alarm. What was an intellectual to take up arms against? People were comfortable, and the American empire was challenged only by "Red China" and the Soviets.

Wilson mounted his new attacks in several forms: historical works, "pieces of his mind," and studies of minority groups. In the late forties he started to investigate the intellectual climate of the Civil War, including American ideas of patriotism and power. Our national convulsion provided him with a metaphor for tyranny, a paradigm of America's tendency to dominate. Wilson argued that through the use of "semireligious political myths" of freedom and justice for all, the North had established its legitimacy and crushed the dissenting South. He attacked America's whitewash of violence and saw the war as the most dramatic expression of the nation's primitive aggressive instincts. He worked for some 15 years to make his case.

Meanwhile, the fifties were a time when he sought other instances of intellectual and political domination: the Jews and the Iroquois were two exotic groups whose histories had much to say to contemporary Americans. Having studied Hebrew in the forties at Princeton Theological Seminary, for the sole purpose of learning a language that his grandfather knew, Wilson was equipped to meet one of the age's great intellectual events, the discovery of the Dead Sea Scrolls in 1947. These scrolls constituted for a time an embarrassment to orthodox Christians and Jews. For one thing, they suggested that the teachings of Jesus were part of an older Jewish tradition. Wilson traveled to Israel in 1954 to verify this idea; the longtime rebel who had rejected Christianity as a teenager was fascinated by the subversive possibilities in view. After his research he came to the conclusion that the Jews of the Essene sect had actually shaped Christianity and that Christ and his followers were adapters who had overshadowed the authentic sources of Western morality. Wilson outraged portions of the Christian community and became for some a kind of twentieth-century David Hume, a disprover of miracles.

Soon after this Wilson started studying the problems of his upstate neighbors, the Iroquois. They, too, had been overshadowed and forgotten, and their position needed clarification. Again he went traveling, pored over official documents, conducted interviews with Indian leaders, and even attended meetings of their councils. He handed down a powerful indictment against American imperialism in his 1957 study, *Apologies to the Iroquois.*

During the fifties and sixties, Wilson became an institution. He collected an honorary degree from Princeton, accepted the Lowell lectureship at Harvard in 1959, received the Medal of Freedom from John F. Kennedy in 1963, and was made a member of the American Academy of Arts and Letters. At the same time he acted out his rebellious feelings and became the author-as-outlaw. During the late forties, he had figured that his income was too small to pay taxes, and he had committed the unforgivable American sin, failure to file. By 1956 the IRS was hot in pursuit of a deadbeat, writer of dirty books, womanizer, former communist, spendthrift, and atheist. The war between Wilson and the government lasted into the sixties; his income was cut off by the IRS in 1962; he was subjected to a series of hearings, which he recounted with grim relish in *The Cold War and the Income Tax* (1963). The book was very unpopular with some critics because of its irascible, high-handed attitude; others consider it no better than the cane brandishing and blustering of a literary W. C. Fields.[9] But Wilson was not intimidated by majority opinion and soon attacked what he believed to be another tyrannical force—academe. *The Fruits of the MLA* (1969) took on a major scholarly organization—the literary equivalent of the AMA—and accused its most revered members of boondoggling and making great novels into "scholarly texts" that were unreadable. For this latest crime of debunking, he earned a reputation as a bad old man and a simplifier of the profound mysteries of scholarship.

During his last years he traveled less. After a career reporting on cultures and social systems, using his Russian in Moscow and his Hebrew in Jerusalem, exploring America's lower depths and its affluence, he settled into a routine of spending most of his winters in Wellfleet, Massachusetts, and most of his summers in Talcottville. He withdrew—with a certain irritability and bad grace—from the public part of literary life. He had a list printed of what "EDMUND WILSON REGRETS THAT IT IS IMPOSSIBLE FOR HIM" to do: besides writing, the list included just about everything a famous writer does do. Nevertheless, in Wellfleet he was part of the show on *la plage des intellectuels*. With his soiled panama hat, long dress shirt ("I have only one way of dressing"), Bermudas, and gold-headed cane, he was an austere reminder of the dignity of literary life.[10] He had endured and was now a monument in the midst of other generations of writers and thinkers. As always, he was ready for an exchange of ideas—with Alfred Kazin, Arthur Schlesinger, and other members of America's intellectual establishment. Yet there was something in the publicness of Wellfleet ("the fucking Riviera") that he disliked. He needed the old stone house in upstate New York. It was a place where he could escape from family and marriage, fame, parties, and modernity.

In Talcottville he worked on *Upstate,* his final reflections on his family and the older American civilization in which he felt most at home. In

the sixties he formed a number of friendships with his Talcottville neighbors, most notably with a Hungarian woman, Mary Pcolar.[11] She
became his part-time secretary, chauffeur, and teacher. He studied Hungarian with her, and together they enjoyed picnics, hiking with her children, and the inevitable drinking. (The erotic element, alas, was weaker
than the old man could have wished.) Mary's place in his life constituted
a point of resolution: he had finally made serene and satisfying contact
with an ordinary working person. Talcottville provided the setting in
which he could reconcile the castle of ideas and the need for unencumbered relationships.

When Wilson died on June 12, 1972, of heart failure, he left a book
at the printer's and a number of other manuscripts. There seemed no
end to his bibliography,[12] and hardly a daunting subject that he had
lacked the strength to tackle. Above his desk he had once caused the
Hebrew words meaning "Be Strong, Be Strong" to be mounted. In a
1936 letter to a nonproductive author he summed up his literary code of
honor:

> What the hell's the matter with you, you old fraud?—why don't you
> produce some literature? Haven't you heard about that one talent which
> is death to hide? Besides, during this ghastly period, when the world's in
> the doldrums, good work is all the more important; why leave the field
> to the phonies?

Chapter Two
A Triple Thinker

Edmund Wilson left his imprint on a great age of literary criticism by inviting a general audience to a discussion of the human significance of literature, by unceremoniously offering his readers a few vantage points from which to look at books, and by devising ways to help his readers meet the intellectual demands of literature.[1] He stands as one of the twentieth century's least forbidding major critics, one who established his authority, not by theories, complex analyses, or exhaustive considerations of writers, but by his intense curiosity about creative artists and his candid judgments of them. His essays have the swift, direct quality of journalism and the deeply reflective character of judgmental criticism. They are dynamic, dramatic evaluations of writers and the moods and shapes of literature. Wilson established himself as an opinionated correspondent on the front line of modern literature, someone who could tell you how it felt and what books meant for culture and society.

A first-rate correspondent must be alert and flexible, yet have some vantage point from which to view the ever-changing pattern. During the 1920s Wilson developed three points of view for reporting on the spectacle of literature: the aesthetic, the social, and the psychological. Although such viewpoints were not new in modern criticism—Walter Pater viewed literature aesthetically, Arnold criticized literature as a social document, Van Wyck Brooks used the psychological method—Wilson used them with an assurance, firmness, and vitality that made his criticism a monument of balanced intelligence.[2] His best nineteenth-century forebears frequently distorted literary texts, turned writers' ideas into abstract positions, made literature into pure fabrication or social criticism or revelation. His greatest contemporaries in criticism often made literary criticism seem like a branch of epistemology or experimental science. But Wilson never let his approaches crowd the drama of creative art and artists off the stage.

In "A Modest Self-Tribute" Wilson tells how he became a literary critic. As a boy he read Taine's *History of English Literature,* a work that thrilled him with its novelistic approach to writers, their habits, and settings. Taine "had created the creators themselves as characters in a

larger drama of cultural and social history, and writing about literature
for me, has always meant narrative and drama as well as the discussion
of comparative values." From the time he began writing essays at Hill
School he also developed the habit of bringing various kinds of literature
into communication; this meant seeing one writer in relation to others,
and because of Wilson's early struggle to transcend his environment, it
included a desire "to break down conventional frames, to get away from
academic canons that always tend to keep literature provincial." Part of
his larger revolt, this attitude made him especially sensitive to the non-
Anglo-Saxon literatures, the forgotten books, and those works encrusted with clichés and stock responses. His purpose was clear for fifty
years: as a reporter he sought to get the accurate picture and replace the
tiresome and tepid impressions of works with an ongoing drama of the
universal imagination.

Wilson not only had to break with the conventional frames of the
past; he also had to define himself in a great age of criticism. The twenties and thirties were a period during which writing about literature
became an extension of the modern tradition; in ingenuity and boldness
of vision, the best critics followed Ezra Pound's injunction to "make it
new." Their works of interpretation were complex, demanding, often
allusive and elusive, and very often based on difficult philosophical
assumptions or other presumptions about what a reader should know.
Kenneth Burke, an American maverick, moved elliptically in a world of
poetics, anthropology, sociology, and linguistic theory. His books are
dense, rich, and often inaccessible to the informed general reader. I. A.
Richards, a professor and psychological theorist, moved through a tan-
gle of theories, and his landmark work on the art of reading literature
assumes that a reader is prepared to deal with epistemology, theory of
language, and aesthetics. Even T. S. Eliot's criticism ranged over bodies
of Western literature and asked the reader to appreciate finely spun
arguments and to savor the judgments and sensibility of a learned poet.

By contrast, the reader who opens Wilson's first major critical book,
Axel's Castle, will be gradually initiated into the symbolist way of looking at words and reality. Assuming little about his reader's literary background, Wilson surveys the major intellectual currents of the nineteenth
century and shows how symbolism is a second kind of revolt against
precision, rationality, and denotation. While romantics like Wordsworth
and Coleridge broke with the decorum and restraint of the eighteenth
century—used simpler language, brought the self as a subject into
poetry—the symbolists went the distance; they broke entirely with the

mimetic notion that external reality is the poet's concern. They eroded the sense of the "real" and became imaginative in a radically new sense. Without unloading a trunkful of "isms" on his audience, Wilson conveys this great change through cameo portraits of writers. "Breaking with reality" amounted to cultivating private sensations. Wilson distills this idea in his image of the French poet Mallarmé, "a true saint of literature," who claimed he smoked to put some distance "between the world and himself." Gérard de Nerval, another pioneer of sensibility, suffered from spells of insanity and confused fancies with reality. These poets sought a kind of programmatic confusion of references: they needed to find words for strange moods, not for familiar things. Symbolism, then, becomes "an attempt by carefully studied means—a complicated association of ideas represented by a medley of metaphors—to communicate unique personal feelings." The poets pursued such metaphoric language in a variety of ways. Nerval's hallucinatory "method" aimed to represent his idea that the world was bound up with our dreams; he wrote of "souls of lonely places" and "a pure spirit under the bark of stones." Edgar Allan Poe studiously confused the senses: darkness could be heard, for example.

In analyzing the processes of the symbolist poets, Wilson also frames his discussion with some philosophical observations about symbolist language—and its dangers. Here he subtly exercises his function as judicial critic. A language that intimates, works by association and avoids statement, changes with every moment of consciousness, is likely to be abstract and musical—a series of metaphors seemingly detached from subjects that the reader can identify. Wilson says that "one has to guess what the images are being applied to." He reveals, despite his sympathy, a basic distrust; his pioneering criticism does not prevent him from assuming the role of a Voltaire among these wild men.[3]

For all his reverence Wilson keeps some distance between himself and the six experimentalists whom he discusses in the central section of *Axel's Castle*. Like Dr. Johnson in his *Lives of the Poets*, Wilson reserves the right to call his subjects up short, chastise them for lapses in communication and inconsistencies, and on occasion, cavil about the way they live and think. Fascinated and repulsed by oddity, he often delivers severe judgments.[4] He is especially troubled by the various kinds of escape that characterize the nineteenth-century symbolists and their twentieth-century successors: escape from denotation, from science, and from social commitment. Although he is receptive to the ways in which they have extended the boundaries of literature, he remains disturbed by their excesses and distrustful, in an almost puritanical way, of playfulness in art.

Wilson's "major characters"—most of them second-generation symbolists—are viewed in their relation to the book's controlling metaphor, the castle. Wilson's organization involves a building up of the ideas of isolating distance, the pursuit of an indefinite kingdom of art. His artists have unique ways of fabricating castles for themselves. Although the reader senses the drift of Wilson's argument, he or she is left without direct discussion of Axel's castle itself until the later pages of the book. These final pages are a series of grand emblems, and they present the symbolist doctrines in a highly vivid and dramatic way.

First, however, Wilson introduces his symbolist aesthetes in a series of gallery portraits that exhibit and judge. William Butler Yeats's early poetry and prose are an occasion not only for analysis but also for a discussion of the artist who is scornful of the world, looks to a fairyland of imagination, and finds reality useful as a storehouse from which to retrieve metaphors. Wilson is sensitive to Yeats's ambivalent attitude toward the world of Druidic wisdom and dreamy transcendence, yet he considers this world unsoiled by age and decay, care and love's bitter mystery, as Yeats's lotus land. It is true that Wilson was one of the earliest critics to recognize that Yeats's poetry was dependent on ironic tension and unresolved conflict between the self's search for delight and the demands of reality. But in dealing with Yeats's early prose, much of which explores the occult and mythological, Wilson expresses his distrust of a metaphor maker who strays too far from ordinary life. He finds Yeats's archaisms and mannerisms pompous and all too "clothed by metaphor." On the one hand, the figurative prose style irked the young writer who served his apprenticeship with Mr. Rolfe. On the other hand, he felt that Yeats's "homeliness"—his ability to employ concrete language to grasp abstractions—was one of his greatest gifts: Yeats's fusion of "direct contact"—the stuff of everyday life—and "abstraction"—visionary systems, the occult—constitutes his greatest achievement.

Wilson is most involved with this complex act of poetic negotiation: if a writer can sustain it, he or she earns praise; but if the writer runs into the sands of obscurity or self-referring experiment, Wilson displays a very instructive kind of impatience. Paul Valéry, for example, is presented with little sympathy. For 20 years Valéry stopped writing poetry and created philosophical, involuted speculation that issued from a character called M. Teste. This asocial, distanced figure who believes that action inhibits thought gives Wilson "the creeps." The forthright, idiomatic quality of Wilson's response tells us how to locate his position and taste in writing, as does his comment on Valéry's discursive prose: "snarled in a knot of words which balks the understanding at the same time that it exasperates the taste." As a negotiator between disciplines and kinds of literature, he is revolted by Valéry's hothouse attitude toward poetry. Wilson, unlike the poet, believes that poetry and prose exist on the same continuum and that poetry is not some totally mysterious and otherworldly fabrication. This recoiling from the misty regions of literature and criticism leads him into a defense of lucidity; it also makes the reader pause and wonder why he has chosen to take on figures who have eroded the very values he lives by.

Answers to this are to be sought in Wilson's nature as well as in the qualities of his subjects. Escape and transcendence—the dream of a fabricated life, the castle of art—were part of the imaginative enterprise of a young man who had emerged from the Protestant dogmatism of Hill, the parochialism of Red Bank, and the country club atmosphere of Princeton; something beyond the life of his class and his country, something crafted and rare was a possibility around which to shape his work. To write about such refugees from nineteenth- and twentieth-century materialism and convention was to become one with them in a heroic sense. Then, of course, there is the equally subjective matter of the qualities that he found in their poems and novels in addition to strangeness and complex elaboration. First, Wilson has selected artists whose lives and works are apposite to his own problems with isolation and communicating: he seems appalled by Proust's self-indulgence, Eliot's declaration that poetry is "superior amusement," Joyce's laying on of language seemingly for its own sake, Gertrude Stein's droning, unfocused pages designed to reproduce ordinary speech.

But he is attracted by great powers of fusion: reverence for the synthetic imagination—a more intense form of the cross-fertilization that he described as the critic's job—attracts him to some of Western literature's most notable combiners. Proust is the foremost figure in this gallery, Wilson's most elaborate and fully realized portrait. The Parisian writer whose cork-lined room has become a symbol for the retreat of the artist takes on heroic proportions in Wilson's essay.

While exploring the contours of obsessive minds, Proust also fuses the psychological novel with the biblical, apocalyptic tradition. Wilson tries to overcome the early readers' notions about Proust's novel—that it is a precious, needlessly demanding book about a narrator who can't fall asleep—by showing how the characters are Dickensian in their rich eccentricity and at the same time emblems of rectitude or degeneracy. Wilson identifies Proust's grandmother, the kindly woman who suffers and sacrifices, as a center of values in the social drama of *Remembrance of Things Past,* a symphonic work in which almost every character is stained by snobbery, from the Guermantes to the ladies' lavatory attendant who permits only selected clients in her facility. He also explicates the novel in such a way as to demonstrate other synthetic achievements: uniting past and present in the narrator's consciousness, Proust moves toward making his persona remove himself from the flux of time and events and become the artist who will create *Remembrance of Things Past*—a monument made from transitory things. And finally, Wilson shows his readers that Proust's life itself was a fusion of opposite impulses: the spoiled child became the highly disciplined artist who used his own weaknesses to create a permanent structure in words. Wilson's version of Proust is heroic, a personality "of singular magnanimity, integrity and strength."

Joyce's combining of the external world with the interior also grips Wilson's imagination. He insistently speaks of Joyce as uniting the naturalistic and symbolic traditions. Meticulous in detailing the life of an average Dubliner like Leopold Bloom, Wilson's Joyce is the poet-explorer who brings in a full report of the changing human psyche, a consciousness taking in the world's spectacle in its peculiar way. But with Gertrude Stein, Wilson is less patient; the fusion is only occasional, and Wilson finds her a self-referring, irritating, difficult experimentalist.

Axel's Castle concludes with two bravura passages: the descriptions of Villiers de L'Isle-Adam and Arthur Rimbaud. Villiers wrote the poetic drama *Axel,* which gave Wilson's book its title. Wilson retells this work very effectively and lets it cast its shadow back on his argument about isolation: Prince Axel, in the course of a preposterous plot, has the possibility of the world before him when a beautiful young woman tells him "to live" and enjoy a vast fortune newly discovered. His answer is in itself the sacred text of the symbolists: "Live? Our servants will do that for us." Wilson dwells on this isolated prince's submission to personal sensibility only to try to find a way out.

The critic of symbolism looks to Arthur Rimbaud as "a dramatic burst of light" in the resigned and distanced world of the late-nineteenth-century aesthetes. Poet, rebel, vagabond, sociopath, break-neck learner of languages, gunrunner, repudiator of Europe, Rimbaud breaks out of the castle of symbolism and into a life of adventure, pain, and self-destruction. He throws up his career as a poet, burns his own books, and proceeds to act out his imaginative life by going to Africa and setting himself up as a local visionary. Wilson is excited by this unharnessing of action and contrasts it with what the symbolists and their successors have done to life itself:

> we have watched the human spirit, strained to its most resolute sincerity and in possession of its highest faculties, breaking itself in the effort to escape, first from humiliating compromise, and then from chaos equally humiliating. And when we turn back to consider even the masterpieces of that literature which Rimbaud had helped to found and which he had repudiated, we are oppressed by a sullenness, a lethargy, a sense of energies ingrown and sometimes festering. Even the poetry of the noble Yeats, still repining through middle age over the emotional miscarriages of youth, is dully weighted, for all its purity and candor, by a leaden acquiescence in defeat.

Warner Berthoff argues, with some justification, that Wilson misses the radical negativism of Rimbaud, a poet who lapsed into silence. The progressive Wilson does not face up to the real antinomy—not art versus acting or an art of isolation versus an art of engagement, but the terrifying possibility that the modern movement contains within it the seeds of self-destruction, absurdity, and silence.

Instead of exploring this implication, Wilson has put the castle before us only to suggest ways of escape. At the end of his book, he pursues his own progressive notion of art: symbolism has been a great advancement beyond the limitations of naturalistic representation, but it, too, is only a stage.[5] In Proust and Joyce it has reached its highest development; Wilson plainly expresses the idea that the experimentalist tradition with its difficulty of language can reasonably go no further. Anything beyond Joyce's experiments with consciousness would be beyond Wilson's notion of art. He predicts a fusion of this new kind of language—Joyce's stream of consciousness—with the language of science; something new and simpler, a "technique of dealing with our perceptions," may emerge.

Since Wilson provides no analysis of this point, we can only guess what he had in mind. He appears to reaffirm his commitment to a plainer instrument for describing perception, an accessible language and one that is useful socially. This language will have been forged by great modernists and reforged by those to come. It is, indeed, Wilson's dream-fusion: the syncretist's vision, a noble reconciliation that absurdist plays and postmodernist literature do not seem to embody in our time. Wilson is grandly wrong as a visionary critic in this book, but his unprophetic argument about social usefulness was fruitful in the sense that he clarified his own agenda as a critic.

The Triple Thinkers, Wilson's next major work of literary criticism, is an amalgam of elements and attitudes. It carries over from *Axel's Castle* Wilson's deep concern for the aesthetic object and the artist's sovereignty. It contains a good deal of psychological criticism, unsystematically presented. But most of all it employs the historical method to understand writers. Written at the height of Marxist activity in America, it addresses itself to the literary controversies of the age: Can literature be understood through a study of the environments that produce writers? Can the value of a work be determined by its historical, social, or economic importance? Or by the coherence or decency of its politics?

A first reading of these twelve collected essays might give the reader the impression that Wilson has unloaded assorted magazine pieces on his public. With the exception of the two essays on history and literature, the subjects have a variety that suggests disunity. What, after all, does Flaubert have to do with Ben Jonson? What does either of them have to do with the American essayist John Jay Chapman? And, indeed, Wilson's structure here is not that of the galleries of *Axel's Castle;* rather, he has arranged his concerns about society and art as they appear in essays from the thirties. This casual approach is in itself an achievement at a time when the more predictable thing to do would be to produce a Marxist tome relentlessly argued.

The title for *The Triple Thinkers* is taken from a letter of Flaubert's in which he says that the creative artist is a thinker three times over— someone who is a high-powered critic and social diagnostician grappling with the issues of an era. In each essay Wilson takes the view that a crucial aspect of a writer's imagination can be understood by seeing him or her envision a political or cultural life. Sometimes Wilson writes in a general, abstract way about problems of literature as they are shaped and reshaped by history; other times he focuses on individual writers. As in *Axel's Castle,* Wilson creates the creators—this time, however, seeing them against dense social backdrops.

Thematically, *The Triple Thinkers* is a group of essays about social conflicts in literature. In the first essay, Paul Elmer More, the Princeton professor and New Humanist, is ironically portrayed in his resistance to the modern temper in art. He is a scholar of the ancient world, but, ensconced in his house filled with Christian and classic symbols, he fails to see the vitality and instinct that animate works. His concerns are moralistic and proprietary when they should be aesthetic. The second essay, "Is Verse a Dying Technique?," explores forces and tendencies and traces the emergence of prose fiction, the form of literature that has displaced verse as a result of the rise of journalism and the decline of sung verse. Wilson's next conflict is Pushkin's dramatization of instinct versus intellect, the individual as opposed to the state. From here he turns to A. E. Housman, a classical scholar and poet whose most vital inclinations were beaten down by the pedantries of a university environment. Similarly, Wilson sees Flaubert's disgust with humanity as emerging from his deeply radical, although nonpartisan, insights into the sordid politics of his time. In "The Ambiguity of Henry James," Wilson shows how James was torn between America and Europe, drama and fiction, the objective world and the "screened" subjective rendering of events. In writing about John Jay Chapman, Wilson is able to treat a subject that cuts close to the bone: a writer of essays who has large cosmopolitan views and tastes in a society given over to moneymaking and politicking. In his essay on Bernard Shaw, Wilson delights in portraying the writer who thrived on opposites: fascism and socialism, humanism and the will to power.

In "Marxism and Literature" the conflicts that Wilson treats are misunderstandings and questions of value: first the actual ideas of Marx and Engels on art versus the perversions of the Soviet state, and then the struggle between short-range propaganda art and long-range important work. The next essay, "Morose Ben Jonson," added in 1948, has a heavy psychological burden and almost seems out of place in a book about society and art; yet, in the midst of describing the neurotic greed and the compulsion to hoard that are part of Jonson's nature, Wilson does trace these traits to the social circumstances of a young man who was deprived of a gentlemanly patrimony and therefore made resentful of spendthrift "betters." Wilson moves into a totally different social setting in the piece called "Mr. Rolfe," which traces another cultural-social battle: the struggle for classic culture and enlightenment at Hill School.

The last essay draws the collection's concerns together and places them in a large, general framework. One of Wilson's grand syntheses, the piece takes the longer view of the historical method. Critics from Giambattista Vico onward have tried to view art as an expression of man's social condition. In doing so, Wilson argues, they have often been simplistic and reductive. Taine, Wilson's own master, argued that the times demand a certain kind of art; in our own age Soviet critics have assumed that proletarian literature—an art subservient to the problems of the mass of people—could be legislated into being. Wilson transcends such errors by outlining a more finely discriminating, syncretic criticism of art and life. The critic, of course, must examine the social conflicts in a novel, but these alone will not tell him anything about value. In order to judge, the critic must depend on his emotional responses: "people who understand writing," not spokesmen for ideologies, are attuned to what is "orderly, symmetrical and pleasing." Wilson presents an argument that has its roots in Aristotle's *Poetics:* that the sensitive viewing of a great work of art produces relief, satisfaction, a sense of power, a "victory of the human intellect." The critic understands a work through historical analysis but must judge it by its design and form, not by its subject matter or politics.

In showing writers and ideas in conflict Wilson focuses on the critic's study of the environment—what Taine called race, moment, milieu— and on how it influences literature. Such an approach is in itself an escape from *Axel's Castle* and the idea of art as pure fabrication. *The Triple Thinkers* implicitly argues that the notion of pure art for its own sake implies an inadequate understanding of the writer's reality. In fact, writers produce in a welter of political and social pressures, and even the most "aesthetic" ones are conditioned by concrete events and circumstances, to which they respond. The 1930s saw Wilson supplementing his critical vision by establishing a new vantage point—that of the Marxian humanist.

Specifically, he takes up three themes: the value of historical viewing, the way environment affects men of letters, and the impingement of psychological problems on a writer's historical situation. He deals with the first concern in "Marxism and Literature." Here Wilson argues that economics, class, and historical context are important but dangerous conceptual tools for understanding literature. Without them we have a vague and impoverished notion of works, but with them we can gain insight—and possibly destroy that which we comprehend. The Wilson of this essay is highly sympathetic to Marxism—to the enthusiasm and awe of Marx and Engels and other socialists for great works of imagination. His masters believed that great writers were a law unto themselves, originals who followed their own instincts, and by the way, revealed profound truths about man's social condition. Even Lenin regarded Tolstoy—the aristocrat and Christian—as superior to socialist writers with an ax to grind. For Trotsky art was not a weapon; the bourgeois past and its writers were not the enemy: "Liberated socialist humanity inherits all that is beautiful, elevating and sustaining in the writers of previous ages." As a critic, Wilson finds this large-minded socialist view of literature useful: it employs a careful, undogmatic approach to the way social circumstances influence art, and vice versa. Wilson highlights the creative writer's role as social critic without reducing literature itself to correct political opinions. Critics who preceded him had not recognized that Gustave Flaubert was no aesthete. Wilson, however, reads his works as politically charged, highly ironic documents that tackle the social problems of the time; he uses Marx's interpretation of the dehumanizing conditions of bourgeois life as an intellectual context for the dispirited, mediocre, stale world of *A Sentimental Education*. Wilson links the two writers' ferocious independence as well: "Both implacably hated the bourgeois, and both were resolved at any cost of worldly success to keep outside the bourgeois system." Flaubert, however, diverged from anything resembling Marxism, and Wilson is very frank and highly discriminating in showing how the novelist linked socialism itself with authoritarianism. Flaubert diagnosed the depredations of bourgeois culture while Marx predicted a liberated proletarian future. A lesser critic than Wilson would have found prescriptions in the works of Flaubert, a writer who actually was disgusted with nineteenth-century man, bourgeois and proletarian alike. Such a balanced and unprogrammatic use of the historical method allowed Wilson to chart a writer's progress, but as a propagandistic tool in the hands of a less subtle 1930s critic, it demanded that literature subordinate itself to message mongering, that artists be consistent, and that the times produce what we might expect.[6]

Wilson handles his second theme—environment and the individual talent—in a variety of ways. Sometimes a writer conducts a complex negotiation with his social and cultural environment, as in Wilson's portrait of John Jay Chapman; sometimes he absorbs a set of ideas and seems immune to all else around him, as in Wilson's version of Paul Elmer More; and sometimes a man of literary culture—a teacher like Wilson's old Hill master John Rolfe—creates his own cultural landscape out of the heritage of the past.

Chapman's college days, the 1880s, are a dark time in Wilson's imagination: the era when professionally trained gentlemen found America had gone hog-wild after big industrial money. The portrait of Chapman concerns a young lawyer-belletrist who spent his life "beating his head against the gilt of the Gilded Age." Wilson narrates a story of a man who would not compromise.

Like Wilson himself, Chapman attacked the genteel tradition in letters and the money power in politics during his long career. Wilson relished Chapman's caustic evaluations of James Russell Lowell's style ("Too much culture—overnourished as Waddy Longfellow says—too much truffled essays and champagne odes and lobster sonnets, too much Spanish olives, potted proverbs") and, later, of Harvard President Charles William Eliot's self-satisfied pronouncements about American civilization ("You can put every man in a box—Smug, Smug") and of Theodore R. Roosevelt's egoism ("Such a genius for publicity as never was—and our people being boy-minded and extremely stupid found him lovely").

An Emersonian individualist, Chapman entered New York political life only to be disgusted by the trimming and chicanery of Theodore Roosevelt, the double-dealer, the reformer who threw in his lot with the Republican boss. Against the sordid background of New York, Chapman was an intellectual figure of elegance, rare spirituality, and forthrightness: a translator of Dante, a practical agitator in politics, a wit in his journalistic articles, a Christian humanist, and a man who hoped he would never say anything he wouldn't regret. Wilson carefully constructs a portrait of a writer whose generous, expansive, and cultivated nature was almost crippled by his age's commercial pragmatism. Chapman, like Wilson in the late twenties, collapsed under the pressure of American materialism, only to recover and continue his opposing relationship. Wilson dramatically presents Chapman's last remarks—the expression of his desire that "the mute" be taken away so that he could "play on the open strings." The essay shows how these open strings—a disinterested love of art and a desire for social justice—might have been muted by Chapman's class position and education. Endangered by hidebound attitudes of old Harvard and the pragmatic compromise and showmanship of the political arena, Chapman nevertheless maintained a course of honorable resistance.

For a writer-philosopher like Paul Elmer More, there were no open strings, and Wilson shows a man imprisoned in his own consciousness in the way a museum piece is encased in glass. The portrait is one of Wilson's most highly wrought—and employs the techniques of fiction in its use of conflict, characterization, and atmosphere. Wilson went to Princeton in 1929 to call on the famous humanist scholar. In the essay he creates a persona for himself—the socially engaged man of the age, a sympathizer with literary moderns, a journalist. By contrast More has "a peculiar iron-gray aspect" and "a curious absence of color in his face" that suggests the passionless quality of his moral and literary sensibilities. On the surface, More's house is the setting for a talk about Mithraism. The great humanist Christian Gauss, Frank Mather, and Wilson gather with

More to discuss the ancient faith that celebrated renewal and vitality. But in the course of the discussion they drift into other areas: literature, moral values, the function of criticism. More reacts captiously when Wilson suggests that T. S. Eliot thought Joyce's *Ulysses* was important. What, More wanted to know, does the work have to do with royalism, Anglo-Catholicism, and classicism? More misses the point and applies Eliot's moralizing where the appropriate response is aesthetic, and this, in itself, is Wilson's way of showing how the historical and cultural context—in this instance a narrow set of categories—can color the way a writer thinks and criticizes. From More's vantage point—that of an anti-romantic defender of moral value in art—Dos Passos's *Manhattan Transfer* is thus "an explosion in a cesspool."

The physical setting of the essay, along with other ironic details, throws More's limitations into high relief. His house is brand-new—like the New Humanism, a radical departure from nineteenth-century romanticism—yet it is filled with old objects, a copy of Perugino's Crucifixion and some Greek torsos, which, according to our narrator, seem to "neutralize each other." Living in the house is More's deaf sister, an old lady much concerned with what to do with the contents of bureau drawers. Readers feel the ironic force of this seemingly irrelevant interpolation as they think of More's inappropriate perspectives for viewing the art of his time. The essay's final detail involves a statue of Mithra at the Princeton Museum—the young god is encased; the museum is actually closed—and Wilson leaves the whole scene of limitation, provincialism, and literary misinterpretation.

"Mr. Rolfe," another well-wrought exploration of environment and the individual, focuses on the way in which a great teacher can make a contribution to literary culture. Rolfe's Concord background shaped his life as a Greek scholar: Wilson sees his prep school mentor as a combination of Yankee homeliness and natural elegance; no Boston Brahmin snob, Rolfe was nurtured in the same New England culture that produced Emerson. The heritage of Concord was "the rocklike base on which flowers of Hellenism flourished": neither provincial nor crude, the atmosphere contrasted with the narrowness and rude commercialism of Pottstown, Pennsylvania. Rolfe's values—devotion to learning, cosmopolitanism, individualism—flowed directly into his teaching, and into the head of his famous pupil. Thus the student acquired the Concord legacy secondhand. Wilson's essay is remarkable in showing how intellectual atmosphere can clash with social setting and yet be a major determinant in one's life.

Along with portraits of writers shaped by settings, Wilson begins to adumbrate another way of interpreting writers and thinkers. He uses the idea of psychological causality—nothing new in the late 1930s, of course—in *The Triple Thinkers* as an adjunct to the historical method. In "The Historical Interpretation of Literature," he explains how "the attitudes, the compulsions, the emotional 'patterns' that recur in the work of a writer are of great interest to the historical critic." Such "attitudes and patterns are embedded in the community and the historical moment, and they may indicate its ideals and its diseases as the cell shows the condition of the tissue." This inconspicuous syncretization of Marxism and Freudianism is in evidence in almost every essay in *The Triple Thinkers*. By no means an original theory, its applications are what make Wilson a pioneering psychological critic. He is especially sharp when he discusses writers whose talent has been cramped: they often develop defenses and styles that further cripple them. Wilson sees A. E. Housman's classical scholarship as a response to the inhibiting atmosphere of Cambridge University: all Housman's life he set himself thankless, sterile tasks in Latin literature because he was bred to a code of achievement that called for understatement. He became a captious and often vituperative critic of other classicists—an example of resentment and self-imposed restriction. Wilson says Housman and other university men of the nineteenth century in England, including Lewis Carroll and the aesthete Walter Pater, "seem checked at some early stage of growth, beyond which the sensibility and intellect . . . may crystallize in marvelous forms, but after which there is no natural progress in the experience of human relationships. Their works are among the jewels of English literature rather than among its great springs of life." This is Wilson's brand of Freudianism: no jargon, no relentless arguing; instead, the identification of an atmosphere that hampers a writer and prevents his best energies from being available in his works.

The shading of one approach into another, always Wilson's hallmark, is bound to be irritating to rigorous critics who believe criticism should have a grounding in a given viewpoint. They cannot understand how Wilson can dare to use such a free-style approach at such a late date, in the wake of Marx, Freud, Richards, and Empson. Even friendly critics like William Van O'Connor have criticized Wilson for not sticking close enough to a literary text, for confusing life and literature, and for failing to prove his points with the rigor of a scholar. At the same time, however, Wilson's effectiveness in bringing together methods and providing enlightenment for his readers is acknowledged by Stanley Edgar

Hyman, a grudging critic of Wilson's work, who nonetheless admits that Wilson is at his best when he fuses psychological and social approaches.[7]

Wilson's next major work, *The Wound and the Bow*, employs the sensitivity to language of *Axel's Castle* with *The Triple Thinkers*'s study of social forms—and adds to these a deft use of depth psychology. As usual he is concerned with how writers create worlds of words and how they sometimes diminish their works by verbal obscurities and inflations. Society also presses on Dickens, Hemingway, Casanova, and others. But Wilson gives greatest weight to personal circumstances—infirmities, traumas, breakdowns—that color a writer's vision, sometimes giving it "a perverse nobility" and sometimes, over the course of a career, reducing it to a neurotic reaction. In form, the book has marked affinities with the two previous literary volumes: the title's meaning becomes fully apparent only when we have reached the last chapter; before that, we are taken through careers in art forged under extraordinary psychological tension. Wilson gives the title a chance to accrete meanings as he studies different "wounds" and different weapons of self-assertion and destruction. The best essays in the volume are highly dramatic chartings of development, culmination, and dissolution. They have a tragic power, reminiscent of Freud in his philosophical works, that conveys the life cycle of the creative soul as a prisoner of circumstances and civilization, a battler whose submission is fearful and pitiable, large and typical. Wilson's subjects—Dickens, Kipling, Casanova, Wharton, Hemingway, Joyce, and Sophocles—are linked by the terrors, exactions, and guilts of the sensitive damaged mind.

The most controversial aspect of the work is Wilson's analysis of the relationship between neurosis and art. Lionel Trilling, among others, has pointed to the dangers, logical inconsistencies, and consequences of equating the two; Trilling, however, is keenly appreciative of Wilson's subtle argument. He notes that *The Wound and the Bow* "does not suggest that the wound is the price of the bow, or that without the wound the bow may not be possessed or drawn." He maintains that Wilson presents sickness as an attendant circumstance of talent, not the cause. Furthermore, in arguing that "reference to the artist's neurosis tells us something about the material on which the artist exercises his powers, and even something about his reasons for bringing his powers into play," Trilling captures the spirit of Wilson's book. *The Wound and the Bow* shows us how trauma becomes obsessive subject matter and how certain men and their works are not fully conceived of apart from it.[8]

The book explores three major questions: the intimate relationship between trauma and art, the artist's antisocial impulses as they are dissolved in his prose, and the breakdowns of people of genius. Wilson treats these questions in spare, witty, and learned prose that, for all the weight of psychological insight, is unimpeded by Freudian terminology. The reader is not asked to examine clinical evidence, but is rather shown version after version of one subject, a man or woman who creates under the tension of his or her own past as well as the pressures that beset an ordinary person. The balance Wilson has achieved prevents his treatment of his subjects from being reduced to the level of case histories.

The wound-and-bow idea is not really a theory; rather, it is a reading of Sophocles that concludes the volume and brings all Wilson's concerns into focus.[9] In this essay, "Philoctetes: The Wound and the Bow," Wilson takes an unpopular myth and play and uses them as emblems of something that he has himself observed about the artist's condition. The Sophocles play is about the hero Philoctetes who is caught up in the tragic ironies of the Trojan War. Heracles had bequeathed him his power, but the unlucky man was bitten by a snake, developed a virulent and disgusting wound, and was abandoned on Lemnos by his fellow warriors who sailed for Troy. Sophocles uses this story to explore the role of the injured, invaluable hero who nurtures a fanatical resentment against the community, yet who, for all his repulsiveness, is the community's only salvation. Out of this Wilson creates an interpretation that at once sheds light on Sophocles and on the problem of trauma and power in general. Wilson's Sophocles is different from the stock notion academics have of him. He is not a serene dramatist at all but a writer whose balance and logic in his art "only count because they master so much savagery and madness. Somewhere even in the fortunate Sophocles there had been a sick and raving Philoctetes." The play, Wilson argues, was written at a time when the elderly poet had been dragged before a tribunal by his son on charges of not being compos mentis; even if this tells us little about his resentment, his other plays are filled with great men who have been injured and who rage against their enemies and their fate. Sophocles' tragic sense as a writer allows him to reach a point of transcendence and resignation. Philoctetes, in fact, finally rises above his hatred and goes to Troy; yet Wilson reminds us that this triumph is entwined with suffering and pain. Achievement—the heroic feats of artist and warrior—though not caused by injury, is often inseparable from it.

Wilson's reading of the problem gives him an approach to his other artists: "The victim of a malodorous disease which renders him abhorrent to society and periodically degrades him and makes him helpless is also the master of a superhuman art which everybody has to respect and which the normal man finds he needs." Wilson's strongest essays—on Dickens and Kipling—flow from this idea. "Dickens: The Two Scrooges" was, in its time, a breakthrough in the understanding of a figure whose reputation had been overlaid with sentiment by some and treated with snobbish neglect by others. Only a few major minds had tackled Dickens; the searching essays of Santayana, Chesterton, and Gissing were by no means typical. The "Dickensians"—amateur scholars and elderly gentlemen interested in fact hunting—had turned Dickens into a cozy pastime; the serious intellectuals of Bloomsbury felt that the great novelist was a mere entertainer and someone far beneath the great modern experimentalists. Wilson took on both contingents by showing how Dickens's life and work were related to the world of panic, disorder, rebellion, crime, and disease—in short, to the world of Dostoyevsky and other anatomists of the nineteenth-century condition. The essay's title describes the mood swings of Scrooge, which were thought to be the way the Christmas spirit transformed a dour bourgeois. Wilson's Scrooge, however, distills the problem of Dickens's own life and art: he is the manic-depressive embodiment of Dickens's own discomfort. Dickens—the Victorian celebrator of life, joyousness, and pleasure—is also the novelist of industrial and urban misery, of neglected children, of social and personal madness. Wilson traces the roots of this ambivalent art back to the trauma of Dickens who at 12 years of age saw his father imprisoned for debt and was himself put to work in a blacking factory. He charts the ways in which Dickens deposited his own resentment, fear, and rebellion into the lives of his characters. The art is inextricably connected to the pain, and Wilson examines the dark side of Dickens's character, his marriage, and his inability to bring his childhood injury to the surface. The depths of Dickens's art—his insight into the character of criminals, neurotics, and rebels—would not exist in their present form without the festering wound of childhood unhappiness.

With Kipling, Wilson adds a strong element of negative criticism at the same time that he develops the themes of antisocial behavior and intellectual breakdown. Dickens's life was shadowed by one major trauma; Kipling's by three. He was abandoned by his parents and left with grotesque relations who abused him and made him the "black sheep" of his famed "Baa Baa Black Sheep." Later he was subjected to the brutality of a public school. As an adult he became embroiled in a property dispute with his brother-in-law that reopened the childhood wounds. Wilson's argument is concentrated on the ways in which these blows destroyed the work of his middle and late periods. The blustering, bullying imperialism, the love of crushing the aliens—all that was a reaction to his own dealings with alien oppressors. Discrimination, openness to experience, complexity, and ambivalence vanish as Kipling truculently attacks Germans and foreigners and takes up "the white man's burden." "The Kipling That Nobody Knew" is different from the injured part of Dickens. Kipling is nasty and humiliated and prepared to subvert his own art in the interests of domination. The trauma distorts the work and only occasionally in the late phase is controlled by a generous and rich intelligence.

In treating Hemingway, Wilson traces a similar course of degeneration. The wound-and-bow motif contributes to the disturbing power of early works like *In Our Time*. Wilson distills the Hemingway essence: "The condition of life is pain; and the joys of the most innocent surface are somehow tied to its stifled pangs." The essay studies the taut and tense linking of pleasure and pain; in early works Hemingway maintains an honorable endurance; his characters fish and hunt, make love and drink against a background of futility. Wilson identifies Hemingway's talent as a kind of literary morale or honor. Using the image of the Bourdon gauge, he describes what happens when Hemingway's effects are successful:

> and if he had sometimes, under pressure of the general panic, seemed at the point of going to pieces as an artist, he has always pulled himself together the next moment. The principle of the Bourdon gauge, which is used to measure the pressure of liquids, is that a tube which has been curved into a coil will tend to straighten out in proportion as the liquid inside it is subjected to an increasing pressure.

But often, especially in his later works, this principle is not at work. In treating Hemingway's failure, Wilson caustically examines the dissolution of a great writer by psychoanalyzing his style: the spare portrayal of characters' moral panic in early work gives way to the slack boastfulness of "Papa" in the later novels and nonfiction. When Hemingway distances himself from his persona, he is the artist of the damaged mind; when he presents "Papa"—the animal-bagging braggart—he destroys his characteristic restraint. The disease of self-celebration also infects *To Have and Have Not* and makes Harry Morgan ridiculous. Wilson's summation shows how analysis of psychological causality is anything but ponderous in the right hands: "The only way in which Hemingway's outlaw suffers by comparison with Popeye is that his creator has not tried to make him plausible by explaining that he does it all on spinach." The volume's most unusual essay, "Uncomfortable Casanova," works on the ideas of disease, antisocial behavior, and failure in a searching way. By portraying a petty, cheap adventurer—bred in moral squalor and dedicated to seducing women and fleecing fools—Wilson makes an important contribution to the understanding of minor talent; wedged in between major writers, Casanova's name at first seems a joke. But Wilson brings off a critical coup in making us see into the problem of personal values and environment. Wilson perceives Casanova's maladjustment as essentially related to social class: the bastard of an actress, he made his way into good society—but was often stopped at the gate. His "bow," in terms of the volume's motif, was not only his social career, but his fidelity as well, his ability to study his own failure and record the discomfort of a life without coherent purpose. His wound was his involvement with social climbing, testing himself against the background of the aristocracy. His *Memoirs* are enmeshed in questions of class, pleasure, and personal happiness; they don't seem to lead to anything bigger. Wilson's maladjusted subject is pitiable because he has not made an issue of the wound inflicted by his betters. Unlike Rousseau, he ignored his humiliations and tried to "crash the gate when Rousseau, for all his clumsiness, had got hold of the lever of the Revolution." In minor talents, Wilson argues, the wound does not sting enough.

Wilson's three strategies produced no body of new evidence about a writer and no school of criticism: neither academic scholar nor literary theoretician, he worked instead to animate and reanimate reputations by searching for the sources of craftsmanship, the events and ideas that inform books, and the wounds that authors dramatize. The three works considered here represent his most comprehensive, least specialized, and most sustained analysis of the problem of creative life. Until his death in 1972, he produced volumes of literary essays—*The Shores of Light, Classics and Commercials, The Bit between My Teeth, A Window on Russia*—that continued "to create the creators." These later works, however, are great examples of the fugitive essay, gatherings of diverse topics that are not intended as unified studies, although individual essays may in fact be solid applications of the Wilsonian methods. They are not so much critical studies as personal renditions of literary issues and portraits of artists done in many styles and tones. In another context—say, under the heading of journalism or political writing or moralizing—several of them are best exhibited. Wilson rewrote many of them and hung them on the walls of literary criticism in chronological order. A few of them—on the 1920s literary scene, on Fitzgerald, on California writers—will concern us as signs of the times, as stepping stones in his journalistic career. Others—on Edna Millay, Kafka, and Santayana—take their proper place in Wilson's larger scheme and should be seen beside portraits of intellectuals and political figures.

Understanding literary journalism is fundamental to appreciating Edmund Wilson. Unlike Henry James, he produced no Talcottville edition of his works; he gathered with industry and a certain lack of consistency and discrimination, sometimes placing minor book reviews side by side with penetrating essays, sometimes omitting a fine piece from his collection. *Axel's Castle, The Triple Thinkers,* and *The Wound and the Bow* provided clear contexts in which to view the big, multifarious collections; they may not indicate the byways, but they are a basic road map of Wilson's critical imagination.

Chapter Three
The Artist as a Young Reporter

The writer who earned his living as a journalist in the 1920s and 1930s was a troubled warrior in an opposing relationship with American culture and institutions. Wilson attacked the pleasure and fun of national life and its negligence and recklessness with the same grim gusto. His approach was deadpan, caustic, moody, full of yearning for something better—but never joyous. His offensive was that of the reporter in the rumpled suit. He had found many cheap, dispiriting stories about his country, and despite his clear views of what was moral and life availing, he had difficulty seeing through to better times. "Hard Times" for Wilson did not seem to begin with the Crash in 1929; they emerged in the midst of prosperity.[1] His spirits were lifted by the progress of modern art, but even that didn't please him altogether. The general irresponsibility and escapism of the 1920s were everywhere—in the streets, the theaters, the clubs, the books. Good things and people came into view, of course: the careers of important writers, the beauty of old New York, the protests of rebels, but the world of Wilson's reporting days was a stale promontory, an America where order and harmony were being dissolved by cash, politics, and fads. The unease and disillusionment of Wilson's portrait of the twenties later gave way to the anger and resentment of his reporting of the thirties.[2] All together, he has left a record of his quarrel—conducted in several tones of voice—with the first third of our century.

Wilson collected most of his work as a journalist during the twenties and thirties into two large volumes, *The Shores of Light* (1952) and *The American Earthquake* (1958). These books include pieces written for the *New Republic;* they also contain material that first appeared in other journals, as well as some longer essays that he composed later in life when he reviewed his career as a reporter. *The American Earthquake* is about political events, the depression scene, and pop culture; *The Shores of Light* covers literature, art, and intellectual history. One other report on the times, "The Boys in the Back Room," is Wilson's essay on writers of the thirties in California. Read through, these books have the effect of newsreels of prosperity and depression accompanied by the voice of a commentator who wants you to live through it all—and to listen to his opinions.[3] Wilson gives these pictures of the times shape and meaning by his strong sense of irony—in the use of jarring details, in the quoting of revealing remarks, in his disquieting way of recognizing the distortions and disconnections of our national life.

The American Earthquake is divided into three sections: "The Follies, 1923–1928"; "The Earthquake, October 1930–October 1931"; "Dawn of the New Deal, 1932–1934." "The Follies, 1923–1928" foreshadows the strong middle section of the book by creating an atmosphere of disillusionment. The settings that Wilson describes are anything but inspiriting. Each scene contains its own special dislocations. "On This Site Will Be Erected" (1925) is a series of pictures from New York City—St. John's Chapel, its panels broken, clock without hands, and lurching spire: "And now, indeed, the office buildings, the freight yards and the factories have closed over it and swallowed it up, imposing a monotony as blank as the sea." On Fourteenth Street, an old, dignified house—its lawn "gone bald," its family having pulled up their "drawbridge"—is an image of death. On Brooklyn's Henry Street there are beautiful houses from the Henry Ward Beecher generation, "but an eternal Sunday is on them now": darkened doors, unlit streets, the cheap smell of chocolate, few "respectable" people. (Wilson the snob laments "the shouts of shrill Italian children" and notes that now "only the vulgar survive.") In the East Forties, the sky itself seems displaced— "like a pool in which a large safe has been dropped"—by a disagreeably colored hotel. Wilson's New York interiors, in their cheapness and vulgarity, complement the disagreeable cityscape. In Greenwich Village, Texas Guinan, a nightclub hostess, presides over a "windowless compact room, under the great glaring peony of the ceiling that melts from pink through deep rose to orange, swollen and hypnotic to drunken eyes, among green and red carnation panels that frame bogus señoritas." In "Thoughts on Leaving New York for New Orleans" (1926), the Brevoort and the Lafayette "are being unattractively renovated in the style of the lavatory of the Pennsylvania Station."

Many of Wilson's people of the twenties seem to be animated forms reflecting this environment, unable to rise above it. Like characters in Dickens, they are thingified or presented in terms of cheap clichés. Some have the "machine-like energy" of the comedian Eddie Cantor. Some are tawdry like Texas Guinan, "with her pearls, her prodigious glittering bosom, her abundant and beautifully bleached coiffure, her lion-trap of shining white teeth, her broad back that looks coarse and raw behind its green velvet grating." (The word *grating* is a small triumph of description in itself.) And other types are presented as part of a general atmosphere of disaster and confusion. Their actions proceed from impulse rather than from reflection. In Wilson's 1925 report, Dorothy Perkins, a sexy and hot-tempered Greenwich Village kid who murdered a rejected suitor at a party, is presented as the slum girl who acts on impulse after a couple of drinks of gin. The gum-chewing judge who presided at her trial is captured by Wilson in moments of idiotic philosophizing: "Speaking in a general way," he said, "the trouble with the situation was nowadays that the crimes were committed by the younger set." He also concluded that "women had a tendency to shoot men."

The most important and fully developed piece in the "Follies" section, "The Men from Rumpelmayer's" (1927), is built on an even more artful use of things and phrases than the previous reports. A short story rather than a straight job of reporting or scene painting, this piece is about the perception of the celebrated Sacco-Vanzetti case. The two Italian defendants were convicted of the 1920 murder and robbery of a payroll guard; the action of Wilson's story opens on the day in April 1927 when the Massachusetts Supreme Court denied their appeal. The qualifying circumstances surrounding the case—some new evidence that the court ruled against admitting, Vanzetti's political beliefs, the Red Scare of the 1920s, the awkward and unjust position of the immigrant in Anglo-Saxon America—caused many intellectuals and literary people to come to the aid of Sacco and Vanzetti with defense committees and literary works of protest. Their execution in August became a symbol for many Americans of social injustice. The painter Ben Shahn, for example, depicted them as victims of a national hysteria.

Wilson's protest is to be found in his oblique and ironic angle of vision. His story is not about protesting intellectuals or bloodthirsty bigots. Instead, he assembles a group of country-club types whose conversation provides an ironic counterpoint to the fate of the condemned men. The narrator, a Wilson persona, is spending some time with two California girls and an old school friend named Ralph in a place outside Boston. The conversation runs to what they should do on their last day together (also the day when the defendants' last hope is gone). As the friends ride into Boston, they joke grimly about the smell of condemned clams at Revere Beach, and they sing (apparently without realizing the horrible relevance) "Flamin' Mamie" and "Forsaken." At Beacon Hill they eat a seafood dinner—and Ralph hesitates to boil the lobsters. The atmosphere in the apartment where they have dinner is very Boston

Brahmin—first editions, a volume that recorded the proceedings of a
Porcellian Club dinner, the "fragrance" of Oliver Wendell Holmes's
America. All quite different from the smell of condemned clams. "Have
the men from Rumpelmayer's come?" is the way one of the girls asks if
the food is ready. This strange quotation from an English novel is a powerful reminder of what awaits. It is a euphemistic way of referring to the
executioners—much like the Greeks' way of calling the Furies the
"bearers of good tidings." As Charles Frank has explained, Rumpelmayer's also has connotations of the genial cafe life of Central Europe[4]—
a perfect ironic contrast to Sacco and Vanzetti. The name, however
interpreted, is at quite a distance from the horror. And this distance is
Wilson's theme. These people—amiable, well-meaning, generally sympathetic to the condemned—are symbols of isolation; they make the
narrator wonder "whether college wasn't going on a little too long."
Their insulated world gets punctured only by newspapers—and by their
own slips of the tongue. The piece comes off as a microcosmic presentation of American guilt and awkwardness.

Another outcome of a court case that Wilson reported on—the elec-
trocution of Judd Grey and Ruth Snyder in 1928—has its own ugliness
and irony. This time, however, the defendants are victims in a different
way: like many others during the twenties, they sought a greater kind of
freedom and personal fulfillment. These two lovers, a prosperous corset
salesman from East Orange and a woman from Queens Village, killed
the woman's husband in their all-American pursuit of the good life.
Wilson ironically juxtaposes the case with the death of Thomas Hardy,
the novelistic master of tragic passion and gruesome punishment, who
died a day before the execution. His career, as well as his fatalistic view
of human affairs, was largely overlooked by the tabloid papers, which
played up the lovers' execution. Wilson the moralist heavy-handedly
points out that the novelist who understood people like Snyder and
Grey and their illusions of freedom is, quite ironically, ignored at a time
when a spectacle worthy of the pages of one of his novels has come to
life in America.

In turning to popular entertainment, Wilson finds little relief from
the oppression of the larger culture. In criticizing shows, he consistently
refers the spectacles to the deeper life of the times—and almost always
attacks the mechanical, the faddish, and the cheap. "The Follies as an
Institution" (1923) is about standardization of beauty: the "high-school
girlishness" of Flo Ziegfeld's chorus is a kind of asexual appeal to American idealism. The ballet "is becoming more and more like a military

drill." The dancing is a splendid affair but also a dismal comment on our fantasy life:

> The Follies is such fantasy, such harlequinade as the busy well-to-do New York er has been able to make of his life. Expensive, punctual, stiff, it moves with the speed of an express train. It has in it something of River-side Drive, of the Plaza, of Scott Fitzgerald's novels—though it radically differs from these latter in being almost devoid of wit. As for comedians in the Follies, the laughter created by their jokes is "metallic" and has "no trace of mirth." At Texas Guinan's club, the entertainment is no better: she creates "an evening without gaiety, of speed without recreation, stim-ulating, directing, controlling, in a race with the excitement she has aroused."

From the same period *The Shores of Light* includes several other views of theater and pop culture. Wilson—part champion of balance, part curmudgeon—takes potshots at Greenwich Village experimentalism in a parodic fantasy called "Fire-Alarm." A preposterous expressionistic play by "De Gross Wilbur" is being produced at "the Hole-and-Corner Playhouse." Wilson exaggerates the pathetic artiness and silly social protest: the critic of symbolist extremes lashes out, not so good-naturedly, at novelty. One possible escape from such phoniness is to be found in "Burlesque Shows" (1925, 1926). This piece lovingly describes the rebellious "Aristophanic license" of Minsky's Follies as an anodyne for the "smartness and hardness one is accustomed to elsewhere in New York." Minsky's is genuine, crude, and vulgar, and the girls, unlike Ziegfeld's plastic beauties, "take a certain jolly interest in the show." At the Olympic on Fourteenth Street, however, he doesn't find the spirits very high; like the spectators at Ziegfeld's fantasies, the men are solemn and subdued by the strippers: "They have come for the gratification that they hope to derive from these dances; but this vision of erotic ecstasy, when they see it unveiled before them—though they watch it with fas-cination—frightens them and renders them mute." The depressed qual-ity of the streets, people, and shows of New York has infected fantasy life itself.

As an early critic of popular culture, Wilson is appreciative and highly observant, but sober. He watches the scenes—vaudeville comedi-ans' acts, a comic strip like Krazy Kat—but avoids rhapsodizing and philosophizing about the relationship between high and low art. Direct and plainspoken in his attitude toward what he freely calls "vulgar" art, he enjoys it for itself—as a release. In his review of Gilbert Seldes's book

The Seven Lively Arts (1924), he is generally cool toward the author's tendency to regard Krazy Kat as our "most satisfactory work of art." He admires Seldes's vivid descriptions of performers, but he draws back from the uncritical celebration of pop art and is even quite different from his own protagonist in *I Thought of Daisy;* the young man in Wilson's 1929 novel eventually bursts into prose poetry about popular music. But as a reporter Wilson is more severe about the American popular idiom. The "nonsense" of vaudeville comedians' stories, for example, disturbs him and seems to be a reflection of "a general crisis: the bewildering confusion of the modern city and the enfeeblement of the faculty of attention." As an intellectual observing entertainment, he has a good deal in common with a critic of the 1940s and 1950s, Robert Warshow, another writer who was fascinated by the immediate experience and social significance of movies and comics but who refused to make extravagant claims about their worth and who often drew attention to their false and cheap qualities.

In his pursuit of integrity and authenticity, Wilson is naturally not impressed by middlebrow compromises. The coarseness of Fourteenth Street was not offensive to the champion of high art, but the middle ground of chic experiment comes under attack. "The Problem of the Higher Jazz" (1926) is about an attempt at musical synthesis, the fusing of popular jazz with serious music. Wilson the sympathetic critic is strangely irked by a Gershwin offering of 1926: although it is interesting, Gershwin's "135th Street" does not "jell." Also, "the mixture of the Follies and the Met seems mechanical and unsatisfactory." Paul Whiteman, the dance orchestra leader, has combined the Charleston with orchestral music: the results are "abstract," not dreadful, but "a little dry, a little deliberate, a little lacking in ecstasy, but very fastidious and elegant, and stamped with the ideal of perfection." Rather forced, rather classy, rather empty and unvital. Like the Ziegfeld Follies, there appears to be craftsmanship in Whiteman's performance, but it is slick and ultimately sterile.

Behind each judgment is an ideal of excellence that can be found in older civilizations and in the works of modern literary and musical masters. Most of the time the control and vitality of great civilizations and great art are absent; either there is metallic perfection that kills life, or there is raw life, unmediated by form, incapable of eliciting joyous response. It is Paul Whiteman's sterility or the hypnosis of the burlesque shows on Fourteenth Street. But sometimes our reporter is possessed by a sense of what a genuine culture must be like.

Two reports from the period—"Stravinsky" (1925, 1927) and "A Preface to Persius" (1927)—meditate on the qualities of authentic creative work; both pieces show how the artist resists the cheapness and distortion of the atmosphere in which he lives. The Stravinsky piece is essentially about a composer who is threatened by "an undernourishment of the imagination," by the "aridity" and "fragmentary" character of the age. Some of Stravinsky's contemporaries in serious music have fallen into "bankruptcy," principally because, like many of the sterile and slick popular artists, they have lost touch with "compelling emotion." Stravinsky, Wilson argues, has continued to achieve a kind of vitality through a fusion of elements in his music; but unlike the slick composers or the dried-up serious writers, he does not feed off formulas and obvious combinations of styles. He is passionately alive in a time when others are composing mechanically. "A Preface to Persius" in *The Shores of Light* is subtitled "Maudlin Meditations in a Speakeasy." In fact, it is an elegant, nostalgic reflection on civilization, a celebration of the order and harmony that had lately been dissolved, and a dramatically presented lecture on art and criticism. Wilson the solitary diner takes a slim volume of the Roman satirist Persius along with him to an Italian restaurant. The little book is prefaced by the eighteenth-century Englishman William Drummond. As Wilson eats, he reads and thinks about Drummond's discussion of style and clarity. Where can one find these classical virtues? Around him are a group of vulgar, overweight, garishly dressed people; E. E. Cummings, the master of obscurity and reflector of disorder, is also in the room. It is the time of the Sacco-Vanzetti demonstrations; the newspapers are lately carrying stories of the Italian miners' strike, in which children and women were clubbed and gassed. In the midst of disorder, Wilson reflects that perhaps the dinner before him—its courses well arranged—is an emblem of civilization. The soup itself, with its "richness and balance," reminds him of "the standards of a civilization based on something more comfortable than commercial and industrial interests." This restaurant, an enclave of order and comfort, with its halfway decent wine and its lack of pretension, may soon be closed by the cops. But the struggle for "balance and richness" must go on. Poets like Persius and E. E. Cummings attempt to deal with the chaos and pain of reality, "to find some resolution for that discord, to render the pain acceptable—to strike some permanent mark of the mind on the mysterious flux of experience which escapes beneath our hand." But the critic like Drummond, and of course Wilson,

must stand firm against these miseries and horrors, these disquieting
shocks of reality—he must pick up the poet's verses, all twisted where
disaster has struck them, and he must carry them further, like Drummond, to where there is tranquillity and leisure enough for him to point
out what form and what sense the poet had tried to give them, to supply
by his own judicial comments the soundness they lack.

As he finishes his bottle of wine, Wilson is warmed by a feeling of continuity with the past; it remains for him and other critics "to work with
the dead for allies," to defend the edifice of art and criticism and make it
"the headquarters of humanity!" The latter phrase, at once vague and
bold, is an early expression about social progress that the writer gave
weight to as he moved from book to book. The headquarters is an
abstraction that contains a yearning for a more organic, coherent society
to be created by men of talent and intellect; the artists and intellectuals,
together with progressive workers and labor leaders, were to straighten
out the twisted life of modern capitalist society by bringing enlightenment and political and social revolution. In the twenties Wilson's ideas
about change are dreams and urges; by the thirties he will have become
more analytic and less nebulous about American failures, more definite
about the achievements of socialist heroes in *To the Finland Station*. The
long gone allies of the twenties essay, Persius and Drummond, will be
succeeded by more radical allies who served human thought and
progress.

"A Preface to Persius" presents an early vision of achievement. Wilson
achieves a kind of synthesis in his own mind: poet and critic will work
together; they will serve culture and humanity. The end of the reflection, however, is quite ironic and consonant with Wilson's disillusioned
state of mind: "I left the restaurant in meditation, and, on my way out,
had a collision that jarred me with a couple of those bulky-pink people
who had stopped laughing and were dancing to the radio."

Although he believes in the mission of artist and critic—the creation
of harmony out of chaos—he judges many of the writers of his time to
be as lacking in substance as the larger national scene and the popular
culture. The "All Star Literary Vaudeville" (1926) in *The Shores of Light*
brings those writers on stage, caustically evaluates them—or sometimes
gives them the hook. The piece is a rapid-fire succession of comments
about poets, novelists, and critics. At times Wilson treats important figures disgracefully: Robert Frost is "excessively dull"; Sinclair Lewis's
works "have beauty neither of style nor of form and they tell us nothing

new about life"; Willa Cather "suffers from an anemia of the imagination" and "is given to terrible lapses into feminine melodrama." Some of these judgments deservedly earned Wilson the reputation of being "a fatuous policeman, menacingly swinging his club."[5] But the pugnacity of the report on writers is often instructive and very often funny. Amy Lowell's work "is like a great empty cloisonné jar; that of John Gould Fletcher a great wall of hard descriptive prose mistakenly presented as poetry." Even directed at a great poet, Wilson's wrongheadedness offers insight: "Wallace Stevens has a fascinating gift of words that is not far from a gift of nonsense, rather like Edith Sitwell, and he is a charming decorative artist." This urge to swing the club is by no means wholly irresponsible; it is informed by deep distress about our unexamined problems with art. Wilson, in his own reportorial way, registered Henry James's feeling that our culture, and thus our literature, is thin: "We have the illusion of a stronger vitality and of a greater intellectual freedom, but we are polyglot, parvenu, hysterical and often only semi-literate."

In his essay on his friend F. Scott Fitzgerald (1922), Wilson develops his point more reflectively. For all his imaginative liveliness and wit, Fitzgerald "plays the language by ear"; unlike the masters of *Axel's Castle,* he is uninstructed; unlike *The Triple Thinkers* writers, Fitzgerald "is extraordinarily little occupied with the general affairs of the world." Wilson is both sympathetic and demanding when he examines Fitzgerald's situation in our culture. He understands the anarchic, postwar America of Fitzgerald because he, too, is intensely part of it: the impulse to debunk official culture, to show institutions "without point or dignity," is very much a part of his own reporting. But Fitzgerald allows his readers to draw an inference that Wilson always rejects, whether in the poetry of aesthetes or the life of his age: "The inference we are led to draw is that, in such a civilization as this, the sanest and most honorable course is to escape from organized society and live for the excitement of the moment." Wilson may find this impulse understandable, but he cannot but resist it. "A Preface to Persius" proposes that we struggle to make art and criticism—the free play of the imagination—into "the headquarters of humanity." His essays of the thirties begin that struggle and become more richly responsive to the breadth of twentieth-century social experience.

The second section of *The American Earthquake,* first published separately under the title *The American Jitters* in 1932, consists of longer, more densely textured reports than part 1. By the late twenties Wilson

was taking an active part in the political side of the *New Republic,* and a
number of events even before the Crash had contributed to his increas-
ing awareness of American political and social disorientation. A short
essay in *The Shores of Light,* "The Literary Consequences of the Crash"
(1932), provides the context for the central chapters in *The American
Earthquake.* Here Wilson explains the circumstances that led to his state
of mind in the late twenties. The "world dominated by salesmen and
brokers" was one with which every individual, from philosopher to progressive politician, had to come to terms. Everyone showed the stress of
living in the era of prosperity: "The orgy of spending of the Boom was
becoming more and more grotesque, and the Jazz Age was ending in
hysteria." The most sophisticated—the H. L. Menckens and George
Jean Nathans—engaged the "debauchment of American life as a burlesque show or a three-ring circus." Others escaped into freaky religious
sects like that of Gurdjieff. Old nativist Americans became more provincial than ever. And Wilson, too, looked for a faith, a way of enduring the
roughshod progress of capitalism. He admitted that, "though I am good
at resisting churches, I caught a wave from the impulsion of the Marxist
faith." Specific events led to this—the Sacco and Vanzetti trial and execution, and later the strike of the Gastonia, North Carolina, textile
workers in the fall of 1929, in which a chief of police and a popular
protest leader were killed. Wilson recorded the first event in ironic, fictional form in "The Men from Rumpelmayer's"; the second event was
"covered" by a young society type who stopped off for the disaster while
at a fashionable wedding in Asheville. Wilson dryly commented that the
New Republic "was falling down on this part of its program." Indifference
and lack of responsibility on the part of his intellectual and social peers
provided him with animus and inspiration; his articles henceforth are
informed by a socialist faith that had been amorphous and undeveloped
in the twenties.

Troubled places that Wilson visits are no longer charged with vague
distress; they are emblems of national failure or folly. His style rises to
catastrophic and tragic occasions, becoming more figurative and dense.[6]
In "Detroit Motors" he takes on the culture of industrialization with
some of the force and verbal ingenuity of Dickens in *Hard Times.* Just as
Dickens wrote of "melancholy mad elephants"—the machines of the
new age—Wilson, too, uses animal imagery to render the industrial
cycle of destruction and pointless creation. The opening section of the
essay is a grim portrayal of the automotive industry's relentless power.
Ford is buying up old cars, which "wait like horses at the pound"; "the

motors are cleaned out like bull's tripes," and the carcass "is shoved into a final death chamber—crushed flat by a five-ton press, which makes it scrunch like a stepped-on beetle." The junked cars are then sent to the furnace "like disemboweled horses at the bull-ring whose legs are buckling under them." They are fed "like so many metallic soft-shell crabs" and "digested with such condiments as limestone and pig iron." Wilson produces a similar meticulous description of assembling: "And now there takes shape on this track a kind of ichthyosaurus-shape that moves slowly with sprawling paws and a single long knobbed-snail eye which one recognizes soon as a gear shaft." The creation of such creatures is a dehumanizing series of tasks that lead Wilson to consider the outcries of workers. From there he turns to Detroit itself, a city with 66 percent of its population entirely or partly out of work. Again the imagery carries forward what Wilson has said about destruction and creation: "The huge organism of Detroit, for all its Middle Western vigor, is clogged with dead tissue now."

Henry Ford is behind all this—part author of the general misery, a cutter of wages, an exploiter, and the tax-dodging embodiment of the general irresponsibility that pervades the American business community. To the workers' plight his response is that of a Dickens character, Mr. Bounderby: "Let others work as hard as he." Wilson symbolically portrays the distortion and destruction of human nature in the manner in which Ford causes old cars to be junked. In addition, Ford's subordinates at the plant are "a special human race of his own." They "seem to run to an unappetizing pastiness and baldness, an avoidance or a disregard of any kind of smartness of dress. Some of them have sharp brown eyes, others are goose-berry-eyed; but the preference seems to be for pale keen blue eyes like Ford's, and like Ford, the men part their hair in the middle. The army of 'servicemen' gives the impression of a last dilution of the lusterless middle-class power which dominates the workers at Ford's." Such pale-eyed types again put one in mind of what Dickens did in *Hard Times* with Bitzer, the albino functionary of Bounderby: they are spies for Ford and "prance in the plant like sallow and hollow trolls."

Wilson's places in part 2 are engulfed in despair—material poverty and its deadening effects in West Virginia, Passaic, and Brooklyn or the sun-drenched delusions of California or the spiritual weariness of Wilson's own life in the old stone house in Talcottville. Something has happened everywhere in America. Wilson, the student of Marx, documents the ways in which Americans have been stranded in their own country, cut off from work and from a sense that the industrial system belongs to them. Each place that he visits yields more evidence in support of the proposition that the capitalist ideal of production and consumption has failed. In West Virginia he sees miners and their families being evicted from dwellings that look like chicken coops. His report, "Frank Keeney's Coal Diggers," shows the way these people—who lived barely at a subsistence level when times were good, buying with company scrip—have lately lost their hold on what little they had. And the United Mine Workers Union—their "security"—is meanwhile in bed with the operators. An independent union headed by Keeney is their only hope against the power structure—the police, Paul Mellon, and John L. Lewis. Keeney, a middle-class man who has risked his own skin, is one of the few heroic figures in *The American Earthquake*.

"May First: The Empire State Building; Life on the Passaic River" is an ironic juxtaposing of places. The new building has mostly unrented offices and is "advertised now as a triumph in the hour when the planless competitive society, the dehumanized urban community, of which it makes the culmination, is bankrupt." Passaic with its superfluous people—the unemployed and despairing—is almost visible from it. Wilson the reporter notices on the Empire State's 51st floor a drawing of a man and woman having intercourse; this puts him in mind of what people call the Empire State Building—"Al Smith's Last Erection." Immediately after this mockery at the expense of an exhausted business culture, he switches to the desperate neighbors in Buchanan, New Jersey. Without sermonizing, he presents lives that have been blighted by the collapsing structure of capitalism. While the business community and government are celebrating their latest act of prowess, the story of John Dravic, an unemployed mechanic who kills his sons and himself, unfolds. His tenant Mrs. Berelli is also unemployed and has two tubercular children. Wilson is at his best as he narrates Dravic's futile attempts to keep a store, his failure, and his acts of murder and suicide. Mrs. Berelli, desperate and alone after the episode, "knows that *she* wouldn't be capable of doing anything like what John Dravic did." What raises this piece above the level of a horrifying human interest story is its texture, a prose that registers the condition of a disordered world; the carefully described setting "seems still irremediably infected with the diseases that blight industrial settlements—so that what ought to be fields and green hillsides are everywhere wastes going bald of grass, and the finest country weather is made gassy and tainted with smoke."

Wilson's deeply human but highly controlled approach to national misery can also be found in "A Bad Day in Brooklyn." These stories deal with three people who attempt suicide unsuccessfully. Each episode has the imprint of a reporter who sees individuals at the same time that he creates larger patterns. Otto Reich, an unemployed waiter renting a room in Bay Ridge, is rendered through random details that carry an emotional charge: his pennants of Bear Mountain and Palisades Park, his boxing gloves, his evenings spent with the couple downstairs. Wilson uses the technique of "May First"—employing the tangential stuff of life—to bring his people alive and quicken our sense that their possessions and pleasures, like our own, are ground down by impersonal forces.

Wilson's two other protagonists in the piece—a Brownsville wife with a no-good husband and a Sicilian skilled laborer—are also presented through ironically irrelevant details. The woman turns on the gas and reads "a magazine called *Airplane Stories* to keep her mind off how long it was going to take." Later the milkman revives her, and the round of misery begins again as her husband Jake returns saying, "She had only done it to make people sorry for her." No one could help this woman except a prosperous sister-in-law who, after her own husband's bankruptcy, had all she could do to keep her sons at Duke. The sister-in-law herself sold everything except a pair of Russian wolfhounds. Wilson colors the next section of the piece with the concrete details of the Dimicilis' life: "clear, vivid, and handsome," they are estranged from their knife-throwing, squalid neighbors. The father falls into despair and attempts suicide, and Wilson's reporting is at its most grim and ironic: "Mrs. Dimicili says that the Italians who come to the United States and go in for racketeering have wonderful opportunities, but that it is no place for a skilled machinist."

The devastation of lives in *The American Earthquake* is not caused by poverty alone. "The City of Our Lady the Queen of the Angels" is a critique of popular culture that takes on the spiritual dimension of bourgeois society. At times extravagant in style, the essay is Wilson's latest report on what has happened in American dream life. While exploitation grinds people down in Brooklyn and West Virginia, in Los Angeles Wilson finds that trivialization has altered human nature. The territory that in our time Joan Didion and Woody Allen and others have explored is given a pioneering analysis. This report is one of the first important American essays on the junk culture. Emersonian in its orientation—"things are in the saddle and ride man"—it moves from fads in material life to the distortion of spiritual values by evangelists who employ the hype of supersalesmen and producers.

The areas of assault are the landscape itself and the inane pastimes of displaced Midwesterners in California. The opening sentence has a critical cutting edge that characterizes the whole piece:

> From the heart of thriving Los Angeles rise the grooves of gorgeous business cathedrals: the blue Avocado Building, bawdy as the peacock's tail, with its frieze of cute little kewpids; the golden Lubrication Building, one of the glories of Southern California, which has just failed for $50,000,000; the regal and greenish Citrus Building, made throughout of the purest lime candy, which has gone a little sugary from the heat.

The overwriting here is employed to excellent effect:

> The residential people of Los Angeles are cultivated enervated people, lovers of beauty—and they like to express their emotivation in homes that imaginatively symphonize their favorite historical films, their best-beloved movie actresses, their luckiest numerological combinations or their previous incarnations in old Greece, romantic Egypt, quaint Sussex or among the high priestesses of love in amoristic old India.

Soon Wilson the sober stylist, master of restraint, goes as crazy as his subject matter and drops all pretense of taste when he turns to California religions:

> Not all the places of worship are sober—many cheery little odd-boxes, god-boxes, offer you a thousand assorted faiths and a thousand assorted flavors, from Theophistry to Christian Sirens. And in that rose garden, rapt in a trance, sits Buddha-like a roguey old Yogi, while pink clematis or purple clitoris rises or droops in rhythm to the movement of the mystic's fingers.

Like it or not, Wilson is capable of this.

The more serious business at hand, however, is the scandalous extravagance of preaching and getting religion. This is one Los Angeles way of sermonizing:

> And there is Aimee McPherson's wonderful temple, where good-natured but thrilling native angels guard the big red radio-tower love-wand and see to it that not a tittle or vibration of their mistress's kind warm voice goes astray as it speeds to you in your sitting-room and tells you how sweet Jesus has been to her and all the marvelous things she has found in Him.

Her Hollywood evangelism reaches lonely people conditioned by movies. Wilson's orchestration of disjointed details represents his best ironic reporting:

> She warms the hearts of the lonely by urging them, before they leave, to shake hands, in the auditorium, with at least three people whom they do not know. And she has recently excited them especially by her glamorous marriage in a plane to the young man who sings Pharaoh in her current opera and by subsequently having broadcast from the bridal chamber the kisses and cooings of the happy pair. They adore her and hand her their money. They feel good about their neighbor and themselves.

The Reverend Bob Shuler, another phenomenon of California disjunction, uses a combination of down-homeyness and tabloid sensationalism. This log-cabin-born Methodist preacher made himself a mogul on the MGM scale by mixing "a whiff of the cow manure from his heels" with seaminess. Wilson's drier style comes back into play, but the caustic edge remains.

> Bob Shuler first made the front page with a sermon directed against some high-school girls who were reported to have had themselves photographed naked. This stimulated pious people to think about nude high-school girls and at once increased his following.

Wilson traces the ways this guardian of public morals influences court cases, intimidates public officials, and captures thousands. Wilson's perspective, of course, is rationalist and atheistic, but behind his disdain for religious spectacle is a more general disgust with the ethic of salesmanship. Another clergyman, Dr. Gustav Briegleb, is of a higher order than McPherson and Shuler. He is Yale educated and professionally respectable; in the L.A. scene "he will always be handicapped by his education and by his Calvinist conviction that religion is authoritative, rigorous, and grim!" What is underplayed is unsuccessful.

The appropriate complement to this essay is to be found in *The Boys in the Back Room* (1941), Wilson's treatment of California's influence on the artist. ("The boys" are very successful writers of the 1930s whom Wilson sees as typical, skillful, but flawed.) Here Wilson practices the kind of criticism he used in *The Triple Thinkers*—locating five writers in their cultural and social setting—while adding a report on the impact California is likely to have on literature generally. This extended essay, which appeared first as a slim volume, is one of Wilson's most brilliant, employing as it does the swift pace of a newspaper piece—direct and very clear in its outlines—and the depth of literary analysis. His report is delivered in the tones of *The American Earthquake*—the American scene most often able to overwhelm the individual, even the highly creative.

The main body of the essay shows the ways in which five careers have been shaped by place and time. Unlike *Triple Thinkers* figures such as Flaubert and Rolfe, the writers here have a low resistance to the influence of their immediate atmosphere. Wilson has a good deal of respect for each of them, but he sees them principally in terms of their limitations.[7] James M. Cain, a writer whose typical hero is a desperate adventurer who carries "his precipice with him like Pascal," tells lurid tales "from a Thousand and One Nights of the screwy Pacific Coast." Cain generally builds his stories according to two specifications: the tabloid murder and the Hollywood script. The first provides him with scary subject matter; the second gives him conventional techniques—cheap gags like the visual sensations of a script, coincidences, and wild reversals. Wilson pronounces him "a kind of Devil's parody of the movies," someone gone wild with sexual material that is at the time too raw for Hollywood.

With John O'Hara and William Saroyan, Wilson swings the club of the "All-Star Literary Vaudeville." Wilson finds that O'Hara's novels are rather blurred and seem like drafts. His unfailing neatness of style does not compensate for his general fuzziness of intention. In *Hope of Heaven,* his Hollywood novel, O'Hara is "suffering from Hollywood lightness," and since leaving Gibbsville, Pennsylvania, in fact, he has lost his bearings.

Wilson identifies the newspaper column, which requires little knowledge or reading, as the paradigm for many of Saroyan's works. He scores Saroyan for turning his plays into slick columns that depend on philistine sentiments. His point, which is not very clearly developed, seems to be that Saroyan's perceptions and sense of adventure and ambiguity have been damaged by California: Saroyan's courage as a writer has become little more than "a debonair kidding humor and a continued affirmation of the fundamental kindliness of people."

A more incisive and profound portion of the essay deals with John Steinbeck, whose biological view of the natural world on the Coast— animals, scenes, and the people who live amid them—becomes "a vision equally grim in its cycles of extinction and renewal." Such "biological realism" appeals to Wilson, the reporter whose humane naturalism has been brought to bear on the destruction of lives across America. He admires Steinbeck's "unpanicky scrutiny of life," and although he feels Steinbeck's characters are often hardly above the animal level, he appreciates his unadorned look at human nature. This stoical attitude will loom large in Wilson's writing later in *A Piece of My Mind,* but for now the approach to life is embedded in his larger concern with the physical setting.

"Facing the Pacific" is a moody, disturbed summation of California's place in the history of imaginative life. The essay's pronouncements and its use of quotations constitute a deeply negative response to American newness. The "unreality" of the Coast, treated in the essay on L.A., makes existence "as hollow as the life of a troll-nest where everything is out in the open instead of underground." Wilson backs up this judgment about the Gulf of California with a passage from the novelist Otto Storm: "It certainly did not look real now, this deadish place where no ships ever come and where the waves move with such an unalterable weariness."

Wilson employs a counterpoint technique in the essay: a weaving together of his own generalizations with his impressions of literature. The result is an evocative landscape that shows how the critic's art is as complexly wrought as the imaginative writer's. He treats cultural dissolution this way: "The great anti-cultural amusement producing center, Los Angeles, grew up, gigantic and vulgar, like one of those synthetic California flowers, and tended to drain the soil of the imaginative life of the State." To back it up he turns to writers like Aldous Huxley who have "succumbed" to "the Burbankized West Coast religion." Huxley and his like "will be lucky if they do not wake up some morning to find themselves transformed into Yogis and installed in one of those Wizard of Oz temples that puff out their bubblelike domes among the snack bars and lion ranches." He goes on to generalize more fully about California as a backdrop for literature: "The purposes and passions of humanity have the appearance of playing their roles in a great open-air amphitheater which lacks not only acoustics to heighten and clarify the speeches but even an attentive audience at whom they may be directed." Literature in such an environment, he seems to suggest, cannot be fully itself. Robinson Jeffers's effects in his long poems are "would-be elemental" and "would-be barbaric tragedies" that "are a little like amorphous cloud-dramas that eventually fade out to sea, leaving only on our faces a slight moisture and in our ears an echo of hissing. It is probably a good deal too easy to be a nihilist on the coast at Carmel: your very negation is a negation of nothing."

The only upbeat aspect of California art seems to be nativist radicalism descending to Steinbeck from Jack London—but this, indeed, occupies Wilson for a mere page. Even in a postscript on Nathanael West, California's master satirist, the place threatens more than it nourishes. West's verbal brilliance is something European, and he succeeds with it in conveying the horrible emptiness of Hollywood. But for Wilson the stunning anatomizing of *Day of the Locust*—a book about bored Midwesterners and boredom turned to mob mania—is still suffering "a little from the lack of a center in the community with which it deals." Maybe, Wilson speculates, Hollywood will not yield itself to substantial treatment; maybe a larger context is what is called for if the writer is to produce a work of weight. Wilson's argument about the thinness of American culture, first used in his treatment of New York, is employed to describe the Coast.

The final section of *The American Earthquake,* "The Dawn of the New Deal, 1932–1934," is still absorbed with the incoherence and senselessness of American culture. Two of its best essays are about houses: Hull House in Chicago and the old stone house at Talcottville. The first is a place that tries to create a humane order in the midst of squalor; the second represents all that is demoralized, outdated, and cast aside. Jane Addams's Hull House is a monument to rebellion and resistance, the most visible headquarters of humanity on the American scene; Talcottville at this point is an emblem of Wilson's low spirits and fears about America.

The essay "Hull House 1932" is, without question, Wilson's most emotional exploration of the horror of modern capitalistic failure. Hull House is an enclave of life set inside one of the most terrifying landscapes in the literature of the American depression. The report is basically in two parts: the first deals with the settlement house and its work, and the second chronicles Wilson's exploration, in the company of a caseworker, of Chicago's depths. The latter section contains Wilson's characteristic exactitude along with his brilliant figurative style: darkness, death, and filth give the report the qualities of *Oliver Twist*—or at times those of Dante's *Inferno.* Wilson has prepared us for the latter sections by the report's opening: he uses the gray tones of the darkening city to create an atmosphere in which objects lose their reality and become menacing distortions. Changing shapes appear to him. Things are all but unrecognizable: "bridges in the blackness, a shore?" or "a thing like a red-hot electric toaster as big as an office building, which turns out to be one of the features of next summer's World Fair." Or the Merchandise Mart—"no Tower, in the fog, but a mountain, to brood upon whose cubic content is to be amazed, desolated, stunned." Like Dante being led by Virgil, Wilson explores the city's horrors in the company of a relief worker. Soon he expresses his sense of desolation as he visits the homes and shelters where the normal order of things is overturned. The Chicago Poles, gone wild after "unattractive luxuries" in the twenties, are perishing in the surrealistic world of salesmanship. In one unheated house a dying old man's groans are all that can be heard; in another "the father [is] grinningly and glaringly drunk in the middle of the morning, the mother stunned and discouraged by her struggle against poverty and filth." The single men are jammed into flophouses in the Oak Forest poorhouse (called "the Graveyard").

The Angelus Building is perhaps worse—a hellish, blackened firetrap abandoned to Negroes. Wilson is not content to tell only of its horrors, however, and ends the piece with a section on street people who feed off discarded food, live in "Hoovervilles," and die from eating filth. One of these settlements "flies a tattered black rag like the flag of despair."

Jane Addams's settlement house is surrounded by this despair. Wilson remarks that things have grown worse since the settlement was founded in the nineties. Yet the house stands, planted with "proud irrelevance." Wilson draws a portrait of Addams that relates to several aspects of his own writing and feeling: she is a convert to rebellion, a figure who combines human impulses in the way that a Proust or a Joyce combined literary impulses. As the child of a wealthy manufacturer, she enjoyed European travel, the opera, and galleries. But after experiencing London's East End, she had a characteristic Victorian unconversion: What was the good of all her culture? Like Wilson, she rejected her class and forged a life, not of doctrinaire socialism, but of staunch independent resistance; she became *the* social worker of the age without submitting to ideology. After a visit to Russia to confer with Tolstoy, she even had the courage to overcome the puritanical master's charges that she, as a landowner, was an absentee and a phony. Earlier in life she had refused the call to be a Christian missionary. Her kind of rebellion, according to Wilson the psychobiographer, can be understood by recalling that as a child she told her father she would continue to live in a big house, but that it should stand among the houses of the poor. Such individualistic compromise impresses Wilson—and the essay carries a sense that the big house and the suffering masses, the castle and the earth-

quake, can somehow be brought into contact. Wilson's dream fusion has
been achieved by Addams:

> Through her vitality, Hull-House still lives—the expression of both pride
> and humility: the pride of a moral vision which cannot accept as its habi-
> tat one of the little worlds of social and intellectual groupings; the humil-
> ity of a spirit which, seeing so far, sees beyond itself, too, and feels itself
> lost amid the same uncertainties, thwarted by the same cross-purposes,
> as all of those struggling others.

Wilson's report of a journey to the old stone house in Talcottville is a
piece informed by wistful dreams, broken pieces of the past, and unreal-
ized goals. Alternately dejected by his own estrangement from American ideals and by the unbridgeable gap that has opened up between
depression America and the wild and free life of New York State, he presents himself in a deeply personal and scrupulously honest manner—the
artist reporting on himself as he approaches middle age. Away from the
immediate objects of national misery, he has a chance to look at his
"miserable" life. For years he has dreamed of "a wonderful river"—"the
place of unalloyed delight," his idealized notion of the Sugar River. In
actuality its falls have been blasted away. The old house, too, is lifeless: a
decanter with no spirits, moldy wallpaper, deserted kitchen. His family,
once independent settlers, have been absorbed by the "money power"
and are now confused and fragmented. His hope of reviving the old life
seems nonexistent. Returning to New York City, he looks at what has
become of him: living in a seedy house "it seems to me that I have not
merely stuck in the world where my fathers lived but have actually, in
some ways, lost ground in it." He writes of "having failed even worse
than my relatives at getting out of the American big-business era the
luxuries and the prestige that I unquestionably should very much have
enjoyed." Here low spirits have caused him, for a moment, to forget his
dream fusion and look for anything at all beyond the soiled, frustrating
world of the reporter.

During the thirties, as he wrote *To the Finland Station,* Wilson was to
move out of the doldrums and establish his own intellectual headquarters of humanity—a literary and historical synthesis grandly proportioned and, for a time, sustaining. His reporting apprenticeship had
been long and arduous, but it had provided him with a firsthand, day-
to-day look at misery and incohesion. Sacco and Vanzetti "boiled" like
lobsters, art raped, authors demoralized, families eating garbage: in the

span of a dozen years or so American culture had come apart, and the contradictions in the national life were highlighted luridly. But still there were "good places" and people whose minds sparked with renewal: from the little speakeasy with good wine to Frank Keeney's West Virginia struggle to Hull House—an uneven pattern to be sure. Wilson would have to create a better one.

Chapter Four

To the Finland Station: Wilson's Headquarters of Humanity

The river that Wilson dreamed of became a book about socialism, a story of aspirations carried along by the current of historical necessity and personal sacrifice. *To the Finland Station* celebrates the visions, words, and actions of men and women from three centuries. It narrates the history of socialist ideas in a form that is sometimes like fiction[1] in its drive and immersion in the development of selves and other times like philosophy or history in its analytic and abstractly reflective qualities. Added to these approaches to the subject is Wilson's strong moral sensibility, the humanistic stance of a writer who criticizes dishonesty and cruelty with the assurance of a secular sage. The book is Wilson's grand synthesis—part novel, part historical exploration, part moral treatise. In its fusion of techniques and its deployment of resources, it is Wilson's most commanding presentation of human progress.

Certain philosophical, historical, and mythic abstractions hover over the narrative and inform Wilson's treatment of people and events. Wilson views the world as a struggle of titanic forces and great personalities, a non-Olympian but nevertheless grand-scale story of war among ideas and selves. The dialectical process itself is at the heart of the story: the process of thesis-antithesis-synthesis, of a future shaped from the circumstances of a past, is fundamental to many of the episodes. Wilson employs the dialectical paradigm to interpret personal struggles with antecedent ideas and to describe great impersonal changes. On the smallest scale he shows us how the scholar—say, the French historian Michelet—used the past as a way of interpreting contemporary institutions. He demonstrates how Michelet's reading of the work of Giambattista Vico produced another phase in the idea of man as the creator of institutions; the Frenchman left as his legacy the idea of re-creating society. Later utopian thinkers like the French Icarians used precapitalist ideals of society to do battle with the repressive forces of the mid-nineteenth century. And most of all Wilson shows us Marx manipulating abstract ideas of bourgeois and proletarian to arrive at the synthesis of communism. The dialectical process also is used to give shape to Wilson's story, a lengthy narrative about how thinkers and tacticians utilize and overthrow their predecessors.[2]

The second abstraction that Wilson employs is the idea of History as a relentless force driving humanity forward. Although Wilson the skeptic is not wholly taken in by this overmastering force,[3] he presents us with a world in which his characters believe that they are in the grip of a great destiny. Many of his characters hold to the idea that events are driven by necessity or directed by providence. While Marx felt that men make their own destinies, he insisted that they do not do so just as they choose; large circumstances modify individual human effort and, indeed, may even redirect it toward building some new stage in humanity's progress. Thinkers as diverse as Saint-Simon and Trotsky are shown pondering the idea of how humanity should adjust itself to the force of historical necessity. As revolutionists, they are devoted to an almost religious doctrine of transcendence on earth; by dissolving one's individuality and working for change, one becomes a vital part of the egalitarian future that—do what we will—is roaring through the corridors of time.

On a less abstract level Wilson sees his characters' lives as godlike contests of strength and will. Karl Marx, for example, directly related his plight as a struggling thinker to that of Prometheus: not chained to a mountainside, but trapped in corrupt Western Europe, he suffered like the god to bring light to mankind. Wilson's Marx is shown harnessing his career to a myth. Marx's doctoral dissertation is prefaced by Prometheus's defiant speech to Zeus: it is better, the rebel says, to be bound to a rock than to be bound to servitude. Wilson takes the spirit of this epigraph and uses it throughout the book to present radicals who have suffered rather than accept bondage. The other religious-mythic figure who plays his part in the book is Lucifer. Marx the rebel gladly accepts the designation "Old Nick"; he defies and mocks the moralities of the bourgeoisie and devotes his life to the study of the hell of capitalism; he insists that the present world of values must be overturned before men can be saved.

But reading *To the Finland Station* is much more than encountering such a cluster of abstractions. The book has an exciting and complex plot, richly textured characters, an arresting narrative voice that judges these people, and an atmosphere that reinforces people's thoughts and feelings. The plot is structured in three parts. The first section narrates the ways in which historians and social thinkers developed a human-centered interpretation of institutions, customs, and material conditions. The second section shows how revolutionary thinkers attempted to make the humanistic approach an instrument for social change. In the third part Wilson speeds up the action and deals with the tacticians who brought about the changes envisioned in part 2.

The book's point of resolution—Lenin's arrival at the Finland Station to start the Bolshevik revolution—is the end point of Wilson's great theme. After almost two centuries the idea of man as the creator of his institutions has been used for the radical purpose of establishing a headquarters of humanity; no longer content to philosophize about the world he has made so poorly, man has undertaken a fundamental refashioning of social and economic relationships. Like the best plots, this one is worked out with multilevel conflicts, foreshadowing, suspense, lulls in the action, and climactic episodes. On a philosophical level the conflict involves the struggle to discover the laws that govern oppressive societies; on a human level the book tells how individuals handled their subversive discoveries within these societies. Will thinkers resolve problems? Will they perish? Will their ideas perish? The resolutions of these conflicts are foreshadowed by the partial successes, the utopian experiments, and the uprisings and rebellions of the nineteenth century. The setbacks—eras of repression, quarrels among thinkers and tacticians, domestic troubles, and personal weaknesses—give the narrative what Wilson called an "upstream" quality, the suspense and uncertainty of a novel. The plot's climax comes in czarist Russia as a group of bedeviled young Marxists struggle against dehumanization and extinction. The episodes with Lenin and Trotsky exiled, their ideas barely flickering in the imperial darkness, their hairbreadth escapes—these constitute Wilson's art of intense plot making.

The design of this plot has much in common with an ideal nineteenth-century novel dealing with the affairs and progress of a family over generations. Wilson lengthens the story into centuries, but preserves the strategy of showing continuities as he presents ideals and values that are held over long periods. The opening of *To the Finland Station* is as concrete, as full of anticipation and foreshadowing as a novel by Dickens or Tolstoy: "One day in the January of 1824, a young French professor named Jules Michelet, who was teaching philosophy, found the name of Giovanni Vico in a translator's note to a book he was reading." As he tells of what one man found out, Wilson arouses our curiosity just as a novelist does about the ordinary, yet significant, concerns of Nicholas

Nickleby's father or the family in *Anna Karenina:* the hook of some specific happening is in the reader's mouth and he is taken in by an easily
apprehensible story. Wilson's first five chapters tell how Michelet discovered a new historical method, how his discoveries were used to
interpret French history, and how he dreamed of social change. The
next three chapters of part 1 constitute a lull in the action as Wilson
tells how the study of society declined and became rigid. These sections
are a minor story or undercurrent, like the digressions in a big novel.
Like the story of Nicholas Nickleby's father, they treat of men who
failed. Part 2 concerns people who revived the humanistic discovery of
Vico—that man creates his environment—and who believed that they
could act on this idea. Wilson introduces a cast of social theorists—
some of whom experimented along utopian lines, others who had a
firmer grasp of economics and fewer illusions. He introduces Karl
Marx, a descendant of earlier humanists, as the book is approximately
at midpoint: the great economist's work took off from the failures of
the people who preceded him. And, as Wilson scrutinizes Marx the
thinker and man, he shows how his work produced the intellectual conditions for the first viable socialist revolution. Altogether this means
that the forefathers tried and failed to bring about change; Marx and
Engels—the fathers of scientific socialism—re-engendered the spirit of
close study of real conditions and added uncompromising precepts
about economic causation and historical progression; their sons, Lenin
and Trotsky, turned the actual levers of history that were first described
by Marx and Engels. With his own portraits and pacing, Wilson presents us with a generational novel that traces the rise of a family of radicals: an ancestor amasses a fortune and establishes an estate (in our
terms the guiding ideas of Vico and Michelet); his sons struggle with a
declining fortune (as Marx struggles with opponents who wanted to
move away from the human condition into metaphysics and extravagant experiment); yet the legacy is preserved and a better life is in view
as descendants take possession.

   The characters who fill this plot are presented through a technique
that Wilson casually calls "spotlighting"—a modest way of describing
the art of balancing great men against a background of events and
minor figures. The arresting table of contents might give the reader
the impression that Wilson is a Carlylean hero-worshipper: "Karl
Marx Decides to Change the World" and "Trotsky Identifies Himself
with History" sound like bulletins about these real movers of human
affairs:

But behind these conspicuous figures were certainly sources less well
known or quite obscure: all the agitators, the politicians, the newspaper
writers; the pamphlets, the conversations, the intimations; the implications of conduct deriving from inarticulate or half-unconscious thoughts,
the implications of unthinking instincts.

As Wilson allows us to hear Marx, Engels, Lenin, he also records the
ways in which they raise their voices above the hum of less well-known
radicals like Hess and Feuerbach. Each major characterization comes to
us as a response to a world of restless inquiry.

But the purpose of the spotlighting technique is essentially to achieve
depth of character portrayal. To bring this off, Wilson first draws on his
own nature and feelings in creating the people; their stories in some
ways become his story. A second strategy for enriching his portraits is
not unlike that employed in *The Wound and the Bow:* he presents large
ambitions and great works in terms of limiting circumstances and personal weaknesses. Both strategies keep the narrative from reading like a
series of positions and theories. Wilson also achieves depth in every portrait as, in the manner of Dickens or Tolstoy, he stops the unfolding
story of a character to take stock of a man's worth and moralize about
his deeds.

The writer who often felt adrift and desolate and who yearned for
coherence and a sense of social purpose in *The American Earthquake* now
assembles a cast of characters who did heroic battle with the chaos and
degradation of capitalism. *To the Finland Station*'s most successful people
are presented as acting in a drama of transcendence. They are not establishing the small enclave of Jane Addams; they are forging a durable
new way of life. As Wilson approaches the Finland Station with Lenin,
we should recall another arrival, that is, Wilson's dispirited return to his
New York apartment, the place of disillusionment and broken dreams.
The Russian arrival is the author's way of working through and beyond
his own disappointments.

Certain characters—most notably Michelet, Marx, Engels, and
Babeuf—are highly charged with Wilson's professional and personal
concerns. We observe—as we do in a nineteenth-century bildungs-
roman—an author depositing his own ideals and impulses in other people's lives. Michelet, for example, is a Wilson persona, and his work
poses Wilson's own professional problems. Michelet struggled to fuse
diverse materials—people from different eras, ideas of different orders—
into a coherent design; he also sought to recapture the color of the past.

The first problem had been Wilson's ever since he wrote about fusion and synthesis in *Axel's Castle;* in this latest book he tackled it in an even more ambitious way as he sought to connect thinkers' work and present a continuous story. Wilson gives us the color of the past as he describes Michelet discovering Vico's *Scienza nuova.* Later, Wilson enriches the portrait further by picking up his vivid image of the scholar at work. Michelet's "early years had conditioned him, as the behaviorists say, for self-dependence, literature, research. . . . He worked at night, and made the centuries of the dead keep him company and lend him their strength and their faith that he might wake strength and faith in the living." Wilson, once the rather aloof boy-critic, had been similarly conditioned and could call up this kindred spirit by using the image of the isolated man at work.

A personal problem of Wilson's—the conflict in his life between abstract ideas and human claims, between his work as an intellectual and his passion for Anna—is one circumstance that energizes his chapters on Marx and Engels. The troubled story of the great collaborators becomes an emblem of Wilson's own nature. Marx the master theoretician has a corrosive wit, scorn for the claims of individuals, a stoical attitude toward his family's sufferings, and total contempt for any human situation that would retard the progress of dialectical materialism; in London he isolates himself in the British Museum while his wife and children suffer from incredible poverty and neglect. Wilson's portrait gives us a monster-genius encased in documents, disputes, and ideas. Engels by contrast is a practical observer of human nature, a congenial companion whose friendliness and flexibility help Marx to succeed. This drama of isolation versus engagement, in addition to being a distillation of Wilson's real situation, is also a restaging of the fear in *Axel's Castle* that thought can blight human life.

On a more impersonal level, Wilson's portraits often dramatize his sense of social responsibility. His treatment of Gracchus Babeuf, a great radical of the Directorate period in France, is a heightened, heroic portrait of a man committed to the interests of the poor. Like Wilson during the depression, Babeuf is acutely aware of sellouts and suffering. The founder of a "Society of Equals" dedicated to economic as well as political equality, he was persecuted and condemned to death. The words of his defense speech have the ring of Wilson's own response to the miner's plight in West Virginia. Our institutions, Babeuf says, are "humanicide." He continues: "The monopoly of the land by individuals, their possession of its produce in excess of their wants, is nothing more or less

than theft; and our own civil institutions, our ordinary business transactions, are the deeds of perpetual brigandage, authorized by barbarous
laws." Things had changed between France's Directorate and America's
Great Depression, but not in regard to the power of capital. Babeuf's
anger echos pages from *The American Earthquake,* reports of people's perishing within sight of the Empire State Building.

Wilson's second technique for deepening his characterizations is a
strategy of moving from their personal traits and circumstances to their
large contributions. The reader is made to feel that he is witnessing a
progressive drama of mastery; Wilson's presentation of the ways his
characters transform their problems and circumstances into great
actions also humanizes his narrative. We are shown how the French
experimentalist Fourier forged a career out of personal injury at having
been denied his patrimony. In early youth he developed an acute sensitivity to cruelty and injustice, "an almost insane capacity for pity," as
Wilson calls it. This made him the champion of his schoolmates in
youth; at 60 it caused him to walk miles to help an abused servant
whom he didn't know. Fourier's wound produces "a stern overmastering
impulse to render human life less painful." It drives him forward to
design a hierarchical community and to harness the talents of like-
minded people. But his often inspired use of his own grudge cannot produce wide-ranging reforms. Embedded in feelings and without any
command of large economic forces, Fourier's thought and experimenta-
tion had a weak grasp on reality.

Robert Owen's contribution to socialism was also animated by a
deeply personal vision of suffering. Wilson begins his story with Owen's
childhood observation: "He was to look back all his life on a dancing
school to which he had been sent as a child and where he had seen the
disappointment of little girls who had not been able to get partners, as a
veritable place of torment." Wilson exploits this perception in a subtle,
effective manner: his whole characterization of Owen relates to the idea
of finding a worthy place for everyone within a community. The experimental community at New Lanark, Scotland, regulated human
instincts, eliminated the brutality of competition, and did so with the
creative, strong-willed approach of a father seeing to the best interests of
his children. But the Owenite experiment failed, and Wilson traces the
failure to Owen's view of the childhood scene: the noble experimenter
failed to see that the competition of dancing school is not merely an
injustice but an established arrangement that cannot be overturned by
goodwill and a forceful character.

The Marx and Engels chapters of part 2 are vast, dazzling representations after the smaller portraits of those like Fourier and Owen; we have moved from a gallery into a frescoed dome of socialist lives. Actions and ambitions are larger; careers are more coherent and seem like sustained narratives rather than episodes. We are also moving toward a resolution of basic philosophical problems. The titles of chapters have an arresting quality that we have not seen since "Michelet Discovers Vico," but now they give the feeling of massive intellects and wills succeeding in redirecting life itself: "Karl Marx Decides to Change the World" and "Marx and Engels: Grinding the Lens" and "Karl Marx: Poet of Commodities and Dictator of the Proletariat."

While no one ever completely bedazzles Wilson, Marx comes closest to it. Admiration almost lapses into piety as he presents the philosopher whose combining powers—the ability to employ history, politics, economics, art, and religious thought—are powerful enough to propel humanity to the brink of revolution. Wilson's Marx is his grand fusion of opposites, a philosopher of actions worthy to be rated with great artistic synthesizers: a dreamer of practicalities, a metaphysician of material conditions, an atheistic prophet, a sedentary activist, a merciless savior. With Engels he "performed the feat of all great thinkers in summing up immense accumulations of knowledge, in combining many streams of speculation, and endowing a new point of view with more vivid and compelling life."

Wilson continues his strategy of deepening his characterizations by tracing the connection between the private circumstances of Marx and Engels and their historical contributions. This time, however, the men seem to employ weakness, trauma, and misery to maximum revolutionary effect. The dreams of Fourier and Owen give way to cogently organized resentment, analytic invective, and plans for deliberate action. Wilson's Marx and Engels never misconstrue the meaning of an injury or miss the opportunity to harness their own experiences to the progress of socialism.

Wilson tells Marx's story from several points of view. The psychological analysis of *The Wound and the Bow* is enriched by the narrative drive of the novelist; both approaches are supplemented with long passages on philosophy and the course of political activity in the nineteenth century. Despite the analytic approach, the book never loses its dramatic impact; the Marx chapters have a compelling quality because they are organized around the idea of the injured hero. The approach that animates the Dickens essay is here used to carry forward large bodies of

material: Wilson's Marx "has found in his personal experience the key to
the larger experience of society, and identifies himself with that society."
Marx is the wounded thinker who uses his Jewish heritage, his
poverty, and his betrayal by other men to define his position. Wilson
sees the Jew in the nineteenth century as the heir to "moral genius" and
the inevitable commander of "the moral weapons to rock the fortress of
bourgeois self-satisfaction." Although Marx's father had himself and his
children baptized as Protestant Evangelicals, Marx spent his life dealing
with the central fact of modern Jewish history, the plight of dispossessed
people and ideas. The young man who wanted to work for humanity,
who had a grinding sense of injustice, is the rebellious rather than the
dispirited or compromising Jew. This spirit of resistance and resentment,
along with a growing feeling of power and vitality typical of many
nineteenth-century Jewish intellectuals, becomes a way for Marx to conceive of the dispossessed working class. But no sooner does Wilson show
us the cultural and personal matrix out of which Marxism comes than he
steps in to question the validity of his character's way of thinking. The
Jewish–Proletarian analogy is far from perfect: while learning and leadership are part of the Jewish heritage, working-class ignorance and pow-
erlessness are unlikely to produce men and women capable of the analysis necessary for making a revolution. Yet despite this objection, Wilson
is moved and impressed by the fervor of Marx guiding his people in an
alien land. His response has the same sympathetic skepticism that he
directed toward symbolist poets: he fears that his imaginative hero may
lose touch with social reality.

Wilson's treatment of Marx's life of poverty and humiliation is a
chunk of novelistic naturalism brilliantly leavened by psychological
insight and moral questioning. In the detailed style of *The American
Earthquake*, he shows how Marx's destitution conditioned his view of the
world. Squalor, evictions, illness, hunger, the death of a child—all contribute to the philosopher's anguish. He suffers from guilt because he
cannot (and will not attempt to) support his family. His lifelong liver disorder, which Wilson likens to Prometheus's fate, and an outbreak of carbuncles make work a kind of agony. Added to these plagues are anxiety
and insomnia. Wilson shows how Marx drew out the terms of his material philosophy from this inferno. The man of ideas trampled by landlords
and hounded by bill collectors creates a language of violence to describe
the historical process: the victim sees the world in terms of bayonet war-
fare, revenge, and devastation. In his dealings with fellow socialists, this
vision made his leadership a kind of sustained sadistic activity.

Wilson addresses himself forthrightly to the problem of Marx's savage nature and vision. True, Marx broke through bourgeois illusions, but he did so only to make other mistakes. On the most ordinary level, his friends were his victims, and his socialist colleagues were often his bitter enemies. On a philosophical level, his use of the dialectic was often a rigid application reminiscent of the theology of a Calvinist, and his idea of class conflict showed little understanding of the progress of democracy in America and Western Europe. While acting as the unswerving opponent of woolly idealists who pursue Freedom and Brotherhood, Wilson's Marx is also unable to conceive of the headquarters of humanity that Wilson wrote of in "A Preface to Persius": "It is exceedingly difficult for one whose deepest internal existence is a wounding and a being wounded, a crushing and a being crushed, to conceive, however much he may long for, a world ruled by peace and fraternity, external relations between men based on friendliness, confidence and reason." Yet this reflection on the failure of his hero's sympathies does not diminish Marx as the creator of an instrument of change. Instead, it shows that scientific socialism comes down to us from a wounded man whose conception of the human condition is at once powerful and warped. Misery and hatred fuel the engine of social change just as they underlie the work of many great writers. Wilson's Marx is in this respect as tragically damaged as the Dickens of "The Two Scrooges." Wilson quotes Marx: "I hope the bourgeois as long as they live will have cause to remember my carbuncles."[4]

With Engels, Wilson's private-public approach produces scenes that also show the way a thinker exploits his own circumstances in order to contribute to the socialist cause. Engels's patience and discipline during the years when he ran his father's factory in Manchester—the ability to subordinate personal preference to the cause—provided him with the knowledge he later used in his great work, *The Condition of the Working Class in 1844*. Later on, these traits literally supported Marx: Engels methodically undertook the task of subsidizing the Marx family and fulfilling all kinds of journalistic commitments that Marx was too busy to meet. Behind this relentlessly efficient collaborator–patron–victim, Wilson finds the background of the Calvinist. Faith in the Marxist cause, Wilson shows, is not so different from the dour, work-oriented attitudes in the Engels home. Engels is given strength by the very Calvinist heritage he despised: the proletariat are God's Elect, and the fear, revenge, and punishment of Calvinism are altogether consonant with Marx's worldview.

Wilson stands at a considerable distance from the fire-and-brimstone aspects of Marx and Engels. While he narrates their stories with reverence, he pauses to express his distrust of the irrationalism that fuels doctrine. Pages of his characterization are devoted to lecturing his readers—almost as Tolstoy does in *War and Peace*—on the fallacies of great men. Although Marx and Engels are great transformers of personal circumstances into theory, they also employ false analogies, a deficient psychology of human nature, a mystical theory of value in the marketplace, a myth called Dialectic, and a dim, visionary sense of the future.

Wilson's Lenin is a man of a different stamp—a tactician rather than a theorist. Wilson calls him an inspired schoolmaster, a man who relentlessly devoted himself to Marxist dogma and strategies for applying it. The approach here—again a biographical one—lacks the deepening effects of Wilson's moral asides, lectures, and objections. The skepticism that he has directed on all his people evaporates as he plunges enthusiastically into the task of describing the dynamics of Lenin's life. This leader is Wilson's idea of the ultimate revolutionary: the only figure who deployed his own resources and the doctrines of his predecessors without sentiment, self-interest, or fuzziness. Wilson seems thrilled by the economy and efficiency of Lenin the tactician. While admitting that Lenin is "bullyheaded," totally undemocratic as he reloads "the weapons that had been hung up by Marx and Engels," and lacking in outward expressions of "humanitarian feelings," Wilson is nevertheless not appalled by Lenin the dictator. Indeed, Lenin's tyrannical approach to party unity, while clearly noted, is explained as understandable given the nature of Russian life. Such perfunctory treatment of a brutal career was to trouble Wilson later as he reevaluated the nature and consequences of the use of force. By the time Wilson wrote *Patriotic Gore,* Lenin would be linked with another of modern history's unifiers, Abraham Lincoln—and both would be regarded as geniuses who crushed men in order to create more perfect unions.

Wilson's characterization of Lenin—despite this failure to come to grips with the moral issues—is well described in his own words. In speaking of Trotsky's portrait of Lenin, he actually describes his own: "In presenting Lenin [Trotsky uses] an art of traits carefully picked and quietly placed, a portraiture affectionate and delicate, made sober by the deepest respect, quite outside the vein of Marxist vehemence and recalling in an unmistakable way the picture of Socrates by Plato." Wilson's portrait invests Lenin with the dignity of a great teacher. No prophet or systematic thinker, he taught his followers how to spot tactical errors,

reject pat solutions, wild schemes, and inadequate views of material conditions. Wilson's Lenin is no visionary; his mission, like that of Socrates,
was that of a qualifier of ideas and a redirector of minds.

It is the function of redirector that ultimately impresses Wilson: the
arrival at the Finland Station was the "first time in the human exploit
the key of a philosophy of history was to fit an historical lock." The
arrival prompts the following clear-headed and admiring statement:
"The point is that Western man at this moment can be seen to have
made some definite progress in mastering the greeds and the fears, the
bewilderments, in which he has lived." Lenin—the leader who threw off
egoism and self-aggrandizement—overcame the circumstances of social
oppression. He stands as Wilson's model of rational action.

Lenin's rational leap into revolution—prepared for by a mind acutely
aware of consequences—should be seen against Wilson's attitude
toward less measured radicals. Wilson's portrait of Bakunin, the anar-
chist who worked off his impotent rage in a series of violent actions, presents a man who is irreparably damaged by his own sexual incapacity
and who is at the same time a product of arrested development: a man
playing the irresponsible game of rebellion that he once played at home
as a boy. Wilson finds Bakunin "a little cracked" and is generally unsym-
pathetic to his fierce nature and to "the purely emotional character of his
rebellion against society." Bakunin's emphasis on direct action without
preliminary Marxist analysis is clearly antithetical to the temperament
of a man writing about the intellectual legacies of past theoreticians.

Wilson's portrait of Trotsky represents a career on an altogether different and higher plain than Bakunin's. Although he is an accomplished
intellectual, a man of culture and ideas, a propagandist for revolution,
and a military tactician, Trotsky is nevertheless another figure who
comes off less favorably than Lenin. Once again, a streak of irrationality
mars a great man's life—in this case careening egoism and chilling disregard for individuals. The chapter title, "Trotsky Identifies History
with Himself," ironically expresses Wilson's deep distrust. The austere
Wilson—critic of self-indulgence and self-absorption in symbolist
poetry—is quick to catch the performing, dandiacal, inconsiderate side
of Trotsky. In his desire to shine as a revolutionist, in his high-handed
way with comrades and women, he is the sovereign self, a man unable to
appreciate the rich variety and value of people. Wilson the moralist
scores Trotsky for his view of the historical process, a view in which some
men are caught up in the onrush of history, but others stand back or
hesitate or question, and these latter men, in Trotsky's estimation,

belong in the "rubbish-can of history." Wilson capitalizes on the ironies of this. He points out, first of all, that the onrush of history—"All power to the Soviets"—has produced a distorted version of the teachings of Marx and Engels. The onrush view has given the Soviet Union party rule rather than the democratic culture envisioned, albeit dimly, by the masters. And, of course, the rubbish can has received men of great complexity and worth—such as Trotsky himself.

But Wilson's Trotsky is a paradoxical figure whose worst mistakes seem to spring from his best insights. Wilson shows great sensitivity in tracing an intellectual's development. He presents Trotsky as the gifted leader of the Red army who understands the emotions that animate men in the mass, who can channel feelings and direct them toward revolutionary goals. Trotsky is never petty and has a certain grandeur that reminds Wilson of Marx. While Trotsky is not a great original thinker, he shares with Marx the impulse to lead men away from the "circumscribed I" of personal interests and short-range successes. His lofty capacity for generalization both attracts and disturbs Wilson. And, in working for humanity and serving history, Trotsky struggles for the transcendence that Wilson sought throughout the thirties—the headquarters of humanity—but attains instead an elitist mastery. Trotsky's pamphlet "The Defense of Terrorism" elicits this response from Wilson: "What we feel in it is the terrific will to domination and regimentation with no evidence of any sympathy for the hardships of the dominated and regulated."

Wilson's capacity for sympathy and his strong moral resistance to domination emerge even more clearly in his portraits of women radicals. Beside the men in *To the Finland Station* are women whose ideas, energies, and fortitude are worthy of books of their own. While the heroes of historical change suffered for the cause, these women were victims of their men's natures. There is hardly a relationship in the book where the woman does not feel the pain of being connected with a man of high destiny and problematic personality. The passages on Jenny Marx, her daughters, Lenin's wife, and Trotsky's wife all have a certain sad, exemplary quality. These revolutionary comrades remain loyal to men who reward them with poverty, exile, loneliness, infidelity, and sometimes gross neglect. Wilson the moral portraitist shows how these women were not only harnessed to great ideas as they worked for the cause but also condemned to a purgatory in which they were used merely as means to secure goals. Wilson spotlights Eleanor Marx, a vibrant and highly gifted woman who took on some of her father's practical political work and sacrificed herself to his wishes. After giving up a man she loved, she got involved with one Dr. Edward Aveling, a charmer and sometime figure in the socialist movement who was as financially irresponsible as her father. Wilson's descriptions of Aveling's betrayals and Eleanor's decline and suicide are among his most dramatic passages. Without comment, in the driest style of the *Earthquake* reports, he gives us Eleanor's last note: "How sad life has been all these years." Wilson traces the family disasters with the story of Laura Marx, the daughter who married a French radical and committed suicide at seventy along with her husband. They ran through the legacy that Engels left them, and both took morphine.

But such episodes are pale when placed beside Wilson's life of Jenny Marx, the aristocratic wife, once the "belle of Trier," who gave her energies so completely. Wilson employs his full-blown biographical method to show how the details of courtship had their significance for a lifetime. He paraphrases a poem that Marx published in 1841, two years before his marriage to Jenny. The piece is a dialogue between sweethearts in which the woman, in uniting herself with the poet ("let us merge our souls in one"), has drunk from a poisoned cup and must depart with him. Some two hundred pages later Wilson uses the image to distill the hellish life that Marx gave Jenny in London.

Standing back from the suffering of his people, Wilson the narrator directs a one-sentence paragraph at the reader's moral nature: "Such pain and such effort it cost to build a stronghold for the mind and the will outside the makeshifts of human society." The tragic intertwining of achievement and pain described in *The Wound and the Bow* emerges as one of the book's statements.

Now in the midst of such suffering the reader may rightly wonder where Wilson's "headquarters of humanity" is located. The answer involves a peculiar aspect of Wilson's gift as a creator of atmosphere. Although it is true enough that the author who was a schooled reporter can call up the details and spirit of Siberia or Illinois, Manchester or Odessa, and although he had the skill of the travel writers between the world wars who put an emotional charge into their places, still another kind of atmosphere enriches the narrative. The characters live without any fixed attachment to place; exiled, hunted, existing for visions and ideals, their deepest selves reject cities and countries and search for places of the spirit. Paul Fussell has written about British travel writers who begin in England with the proposition "I Hate It Here."[5] Wilson's people hate it everywhere. He gives considerable attention to Lenin's

remark that London is "their" city. Wilson shows how most of the
places, like the California and New York of *Earthquake,* belong to the
bourgeoisie; but while the culture of Western Europe exudes the noxious
fumes of exploitation, Wilson succeeds in spotlighting spiritual places
where writers and actors have felt the exaltation of intellectual discovery
and fulfillment. Wilson uses several locations—unspectacular in themselves—as symbols of affirmation. Engels took Marx to Manchester in
1845, and Wilson creates this scene:

> He reminded him a quarter of a century later how they had used to look
> out through the colored panes of the bay-window of the Manchester
> library on weather that was always fine. It had been the light of that
> human intellect which they felt was now coming to maturity and which
> vindicates the dignity of man, in the midst of that inhuman horror of
> filthiness and deformity and disease that hemmed the city in.

The light of human intellect—emblemized by a window in one of
Europe's most horrifying cities—is what gives hope. Similarly, in "Karl
Marx Dies at His Desk," Wilson presents the end of a career where one
place counted: "He had often gotten up from his bed, and gone to his
study and sat down at his work table." The workplace is a motif in the
book, a recurring spot where the master creates order. Wilson quotes
one passage from a police agent that shows Marx working in the midst
of children's playthings. He takes pleasure in the idea that Marx "liked
to play games with his children and is said to have written several of the
biting pages of *The Eighteenth Brumaire of Louis Napoleon* while they were
sitting behind him playing horse, and whipping him to giddap." Elsewhere Marx's study is shown stacked with documents, all of which
respond to his command. Wilson's great feeling for the concrete leads
the reader into the spiritual ideal of human struggle.

Wilson's headquarters of humanity—a rational dream of human
progress and fulfillment—radiates off places where human beings resist
oppression and distraction. Lenin's boyhood home becomes a kind of
holy place, an oasis of culture, plain living, and high thinking, a place
that reminds Wilson of the solidity of Concord. Wilson emphasizes its
universality, its un-Slavic atmosphere of reason and balance. He creates
an intellectual location much like the one in "Mr. Rolfe"—a legacy to
generations of men and women who work for serious ideas and humane
causes. (Those who do not share Wilson's vision may be chilled to hear
that Lenin's house is appointed "much like your grandmother's house.")

At the end there is also the sealed car that took Lenin through German territory. It is typical of Wilson that the 1971 preface to his book—his last words on the subject—should have made note of the fact that this sacred train car contained not only Lenin's wife and select comrades but his mistress as well. As for the Finland Station—"appropriate to a provincial town rather than splendors of a capital"—it is the unpicturesque end of the struggle that Wilson set himself the task of portraying.

Some critics want everything from an author who dares to have Wilson's ambitions. Malcolm Cowley, for example, wanted time spent on subsequent Soviet corruption; he speaks of Wilson's responsibilities in "From the Finland Station."[6] But as Leonard Kriegel has suggested, Wilson's feelings of outrage about Stalinism can be found throughout the book in the attitude toward the swindle of power politics.[7] Even Wilson's portrait of Lenin, deficient as it is in analysis of failings, is laced with critical language and never vehement in the manner typical of the Marxist ideologue,[8] and Trotsky, the hero of many intellectuals of the period, is treated critically for his deficiencies as a human being. If there is any doubt about Wilson's moral position, "Marxism at the End of the Thirties" (1941) soundly maintains that the dictatorship of the proletariat guarantees happiness only for the dictators. *To the Finland Station*—in its sensitive questioning, its hatred of brutality, and its reverence for individual effort—has already said as much.

Chapter Five

Wilson the Novelist:
Rita and Daisy, Imogene and Anna

Wilson's two novels—*I Thought of Daisy* and *Memoirs of Hecate County*—
are separated by some 17 years. When placed side by side, they suggest
enduring themes as well as Wilson's enormous leap forward as an
imaginative writer. With three major critical works coming between
them, they also suggest that writing about literature and historical figures can deepen the vision of a fiction writer. *Hecate County* has a sure-
ness, a searching attitude, and a thoroughness of notation that come
from a writer who has understood and dramatically portrayed scores of
people in his work as a critic. Like *To the Finland Station,* it moves
between the public and private selves, engaging us in the way that intimate life forms a social self. The book is also charged by Wilson's frustrated pursuit of autonomy and social order; its often dispirited attitude is a kind of return to the moods of *The American Earthquake.*
Concerned with an art critic's enchantment with two women, *Hecate
County* carries forward from *Axel's Castle* ideas of isolation and obsession; along with *The Triple Thinkers,* it presents environment as the
major determinant in the formation of the artist's career. Finally, the
book explores disease, neurosis, and sexual maladjustment in the vein
of *The Wound and the Bow.*

I Thought of Daisy, coming before Wilson's critical achievements, is a
weak solution of these ideas and problems, a diluted version of what he
will explore in depth in the coming years. Its deficiencies as a novel arise
from the usual problems that beset young novelists as well as from particular circumstances that pertain to Wilson. Like many young writers,
Wilson is absorbed with his protagonist and with women; like the
weaker chroniclers of sentimental educations, he insists on his women's
special qualities but fails to dramatize them. His special problem is
related to his talent as an essayist and journalist. Pages of idea mongering, ruminating, and argumentation destroy the rhythms of the work.
Ironically, this fault enriches *To the Finland Station,* in which the asides
and lectures deepen his vision; here they often seem unrelated to his

characters, as if the narrator is working through some intellectual difficulty and vaguely connecting it with his people.

As Wilson indicated in a 1953 preface, *Daisy* is very much influenced by Joyce and Proust, which is to say that it concerns shifting perceptions of social reality and the artist's attempt to create a coherent and sustaining world for himself out of the chaos of modern life. Wilson has recycled a fundamental conflict of modern literature by employing a serious and insightful young protagonist who is out to discover Joyce's "fair courts of life"—in this case bohemia, Broadway, and beautiful New York women. Later, like a host of his fictional cousins, he is disillusioned and about to dedicate himself to creating artistic sketches of what he has seen. In a 1929 letter Wilson describes the novel as "a pattern of ideas," the action of which takes place "on the plane of the intelligence."

The action opens as a young man is about to go to a Greenwich Village party. Our narrator-protagonist has had it with middle-class compromise and hypocrisy and is lately taking his cues from a leftist school friend, Hugo Bamman, a writer and staunch opponent of the genteel tradition in life and letters. Our narrator, who "in those days shared Hugo's enthusiasm for sociological documentation," plunges into a room of disparate types: affluent, venal people like his obnoxious host Ray Coleman; an artist designing sets for a ballet of the *Iliad;* and a poet, the intriguing Rita Cavanaugh, modeled on Edna St. Vincent Millay.[1] Coleman's showgirl mistress, Daisy, gives color to the evening by turning on her recording of "Mamie Rose" while the dramatic Rita is reading her poetry. Later on, our narrator goes off with Rita, and they talk the night away. Part 2 consists of a few scenes in which they fight over his supposed failure to understand her nature. Stung by her words and soon left to himself, he thinks of Daisy and proceeds to her apartment where things are rather chaotic. So begins an off-and-on relationship—this time with a frank and cute American girl who seems a lot less neurotic than Rita and the rest of the Village set. Part 3 finds the narrator in a rather stale condition—floating from party to party and much upset, understandably, about the "aimlessness and uselessness" of his life. The pseudointellectuals, poseurs, and phonies he has met make him wonder about the life of the mind in our time. Isn't even a work of art an expression of our animal condition and our limited, determined, mechanical nature? To make matters worse, Daisy has meanwhile slit her wrist, and Rita prefers the venal Coleman. This depressing section ends as the narrator lashes out at an Italian speakeasy owner and winds up on the floor. In section 4 our protagonist makes a visit to his old pro-

fessor, an ironic humanist who offers him an example of the durable creative self. After this restorative episode, he visits Daisy and her poet
lover, Pete Bird; they have abandoned New York for a time, and the narrator derives some comfort from their simple country existence. Here he
also recognizes his own shortcomings—particularly his spleen and his
depressed view of the world—as he once again thinks of Daisy and
basks in her kindly presence. The novel's most vivid scene is the con-
cluding trip that the narrator and Daisy make to Coney Island. This
New York idyll—complete with shore dinner and visits to Noah's Ark
and the house of horrors—resolves the narrator's conflict about the
world's staleness and his own inertia. Daisy—who exemplifies the
American spirit of determination, renewal, and self-creation—impresses
the narrator as a subject worth preserving in prose. Like a New York
Proust, he ends with a promise of his future mission: "By the way of literature itself I should break through into the real world."

Our garrulous narrator tells us how to regard his story. On one occasion he considered writing a satire about the grotesque types he has met:

> I found that my satire was boring me, and that it also went against my
> conscience. My portrait of the demon poet had been a caricature of Pete
> Bird, and I had now no real desire to caricature Pete. On the contrary, I
> liked him. I found that I did not want to write a satire: to satirize
> humanity was to slander it, and I no longer thought so ill of humanity.

Wilson's story, like his persona's literary plan, is about "people who had
disliked their lives as much as I had." He tells us that "moral problems,
I saw now, were too complicated, and human nature too delicate a matter, to be hacked by the axe of satire." What we get instead is a novel of
sentiment and social ideas.

As with many such novels, we receive the impression that Wilson's
people are often moved around like so many counters for the purpose of
exploring abstractions. Except for Daisy, they tend to have short life
spans as credible characters. Rita Cavanaugh has some vibrant moments
and good lines, but she remains rather flimsy as a creation. Her appearance—a mixture of shabbiness and dignity, frankness and affectation—
makes her an immediately arresting figure. But after a few appearances
in the first three sections, she appears as a memory, an image from her
poems, or a rumination about art. Sometimes this method succeeds: her
poems—which our narrator describes as combining an austere classicism
with the most ordinary subject matter—have a poignant quality that

generates feeling in her admirer and in us. Maimed children in the midst of life's routine, a corpse hidden near a group of people sitting around a fire: the haunting combinations stay with us, but they compete with a lot of lecturing.

We are told how Rita feels that "any great strength or excellence of character must be, by its very nature, incompatible with qualities of other kinds—that it carries with it weaknesses and ignominies inseparable from excellence and strength." (This foreshadowing of the wound theme inundates a whole section of the book.) And meanwhile Rita is assigned the task of carrying these generalities without any dramatization of her life. Talk about excellence and strength soon becomes a series of musings about Rita's "sportsman's code." While the narrator is in his early bedazzled phase, the reader still has trouble swallowing the romantic clichés that he dishes out about this still vague woman. Then there is Rita's heroic artistic renunciation: she must forsake "comfort, security, children, the protection and devotion of a husband, even simple comradeship and affection"; she will become "an outlaw living from hand to mouth, always poor and often ill, bedevilled day and night by all the persons she no longer had the energy to excite to her own pitch of incandescence." One problem with this rebel theme—an idea that Wilson treats in the characters of Rimbaud and Dickens—is that he has not devised anything particularly rebellious for Rita to do. She remains a talking bohemian, hardly a Rimbaud in radical negativism and certainly no Dickens in a quarrel with civilization.

There is a certain insistence in the narrator's descriptions of Rita's uniqueness that is disconsonant with the rather brittle figure we are presented, and, let it be said, no irony is intended here. As a first attempt to portray Edna Millay, Rita is a recollection without the tranquillity and controlled observation that Wilson would have at his command in his 1948 essay about Edna.[2] In addition there is the problem of the protagonist's last-minute acceptance of the woman who has wounded him. He feels better about her because of a sonnet she has sent him from Paris, a bad poem that commemorates their old love. Maybe the poem isn't so bad; maybe he should think better of humanity, too. This is all rather abrupt and forced, part of the yea-saying tendency in the novel's conclusion. Unlike the affirmations in *To the Finland Station,* it is altogether too neat.

Daisy, by contrast, is a character whose behavior has an autonomous, vital quality that does not have to be clumsily adjusted to the novel's ideas. Her scenes are uniformly distributed throughout the book, and in each of them Wilson's ruminations, while sometimes essayistic, are at least in keeping with her nature. Her value is also not so highly dependent on musings, and in many ways her goofy, unreflective life provides more substance than Rita's posturings. While Rita's presence expresses the dignity of art, Daisy is a Broadway chorus girl and jazz baby, filled not with poetry, but with wisecracks and intuitions. While even Rita's enjoyment has a tormented quality, Daisy's troubles with men, drink, and work always have an admixture of humor and incongruity. While Rita's pleasure-denying nature produces art, Daisy's love of fun produces the novel's strongest moments and most satisfying insights about America.

Through Daisy's words and antics, Wilson offers an alternative to suffering artists and the world of the castle. She is spontaneity as opposed to conscious fabrication, impulse rather than reflection. The experience of being with Daisy is a way of coming to grips with the American idiom. The "coarseness and sharpness" of Daisy's slang—enchanting to our protagonist—relates to the combinations that are powerful forces in life and art. Observing the way she talks—"out of that sprawling square-syllabled speech where the words had been like colorless frame-houses on the outskirts of an American town"—is in itself a breakthrough for an intellectual living at a distance from ordinary people. Daisy's record of "Mamie Rose"—at first hearing, a squawky fox-trot and later on, when the narrator is depressed, a hideous commentary on disorder—becomes finally a piece that combines traditions, and constitutes an authentic kind of art. Like Daisy, the song is a mixture of the acrid and the sweet and at first seems cheap. Wilson's characteristic musings are used here to good effect as they describe the value of the popular culture: "an aliment, a stimulant, as natural and necessary as food and drink themselves!"

Daisy is always there when the narrator breaks through into life. He goes to the movies with her. Putting aside his politics and his critical nature, he enters a world of pleasure and pure childish sensation. The thrill of the ordinary soon is rendered in Wilson's oddly sensuous language: as he holds her tired feet in his hands after they have returned to her place, he describes them as being "like two little moist cream cheeses encased in covers of cloth." Later, on the boat to Coney Island, the protagonist describes "the luxuriance and rankness of America"—a Joycean epiphany, a moment when the everyday world projects itself in an image on the artist's consciousness. And, finally, the romantic nimbus in which he has always surrounded women is dispelled. Daisy once told him that she rode on a motorcycle to Atlantic City after a spectacular elopement with her first husband. Our narrator—the one who embroidered Rita—is captivated by such an all-American bicycle built for two. She finally tells him that she was pregnant and that the idyll was just the man's way of causing her to abort. All of which says that Daisy is the resilient, demystified American girl—not out of a ladies' magazine of the twenties and not a chic product of the Village.

Several men have also contributed to the narrator's development and recognitions. Hugo Bamman, a model of rectitude and integrity, is an intellectual with revolutionary sentiments whose successful novels are built on frustrations and denials not unlike Rita's, and whose life is very much like the strained and emotionally distanced way of life Wilson was trying to break out of. Hugo—the bourgeois-baiting leftist of good family—has devoted himself to seeking Wilson's headquarters of humanity; relentlessly compassionate and idealistic, he is also intransigent and isolated.

While struggling to shake off Hugo's majestic kind of rebelliousness, our narrator finds Hugo to be a solid worker in a world of insubstantial people. Hugo is the professional author, a man who works with the assiduousness and ambition of a doctor or lawyer. The establishment of some sound professional purpose—in this case writing a book—is what our narrator is seeking. Hugo's father has also played a part in influencing his development: this acerbic oddball, partially modeled on Wilson's father, talks to teenagers about literature "as if Shakespeare belonged to the same world as the United States; as if he, John Ellison Bamman, belonged to the world of history and literature, and as if he took it for granted that we, since he talked to us as equals, might hope to belong to it, too; as if, in fact, that world were our world." This genial and imaginative way of dealing with literature—an early description of Wilson's own linking of literature with the concerns of men—"finally supplies a connection between the private thoughts and emotions, and the names and legends, of youth." Remembering the spirit of this man is another way of breaking into life.

But the protagonist needs more than Daisy's vitality and Bamman's fortitude and imagination to build a sturdier self. He has suffered intellectually as well as emotionally. He has come up against types like Larry Mickler, a cynical ad man who proposes toasts to Dostoyevsky and seems to wallow in the anarchy and negativism of modern life and art. Larry and other escapists and aesthetes have "the gratified conviction that there was no kind of discreditable behavior which imagination might not redeem." In a long reflective passage, Wilson's persona hits rock bottom as he is tempted to regard literature as imposture—a mere cover-up of authors' neuroses, a "self-protective reflex," an attempt to create a factitious harmony out of the chaos of life. The age-old suspicion that the creative artist is a falsifier has descended on him, infecting his view of the value of work. In *The Wound and the Bow* and *To the Finland Station,* Wilson will clarify his attitude toward this idea: art of course is not an imposture or a reflex but a victory over circumstances. Here, however, Wilson's character needs some anodyne for his pain.

Fortunately, such intellectual first aid is only a train ride away at the home of Professor Grosbeake, a discoursing exemplar modeled partially on Alfred North Whitehead, partially on Christian Gauss.[3] Grosbeake possesses something called "divine irony," the ability to evaluate men and affairs without being narrow. His view of American life is not jaundiced like the views of Hugo, Rita, or Larry, and he is of course not given to the unreflective enthusiasm of Daisy. This mandarin, our narrator is astonished to discover, actually sees value in the American business ethos. His mind, rather than parceling reality into discrete boxes and living in one of them, is capable of viewing the American scene organically. He can see the whole network of economic, moral, and aesthetic relationships, and such vision—achieved in moments of "divine revelation"—constitutes a resolution of man's conflict with life's disorder. Life comes together, as it has always for philosophers capable of seeing unities, and Wilson's protagonist feels the exaltation of sharing Grosbeake's insight.

I Thought of Daisy works through the narrator's doubts and twenties-style disillusionments. He comes out believing in human possibility and rejecting nihilism and the ethos of the artist as sufferer. Wilson's contemporary, Floyd Dell, explored similar territory in a work of cultural history called *Intellectual Vagabondage.* The book is concerned with the young people of the early twentieth century, their rebellions, their flight from the bourgeoisie, and their self-delusions; it is quite ironic and pungent about the very subjects that Wilson tackles with such seriousness: liberated women and men unsure of their own identities, the rejection of middle-class marriage, and the vertigo that comes of living with the latest ideas and fads. Wilson's protagonist, a man without a steady job, breaks into the real world through the artificial device of "thinking" of Daisy and resolving to write about her. Dell, however, treats such people more frankly: "We artists had at last discovered how to face life, and yet evade its human responsibilities."[4] Responsibilities and consequences are not really faced in *Daisy:* the book remains half an intellectual vagabondage, half an emotional idyll.

Memoirs of Hecate County, which appeared in 1946, registers a writer's response to the Depression, the rise and fall of the American left, the dishonesty of intellectuals, the commercial exploitation of talent and ideas, and the uglier aspects in the lives of girls not unlike Daisy. During the thirties Wilson had also experienced suburban life, with its increasingly absurd folkways, when he lived for periods in Stamford, Connecticut. He had seen various kinds of separation—Americans cut off from the life of their ancestors by urban conditions, social classes dramatically set apart from one another by the Crash, artists drifting from their missions into the world of Madison Avenue. Social and economic pressures of enormous complexity and moral significance trouble the characters in *Hecate County.* Whereas *Daisy* is essentially concerned with the way in which men and women should think and feel about art and life, *Hecate County* is often concerned with people struggling to survive the new American separations. *Hecate County* comes in the wake of great failures, and its author's dismal brilliance is that of a man who has put together a world of meaning and coherence in *To the Finland Station* but who can see only fragmentation on the new landscape.[5] Sherman Paul has insightfully remarked that the Finland Station—the hope of the thirties—opens on Hecate County—the hangover after the revolution. [6]

One of the places marked by the extravagance and corruption of the moneyed classes, Hecate County is for Wilson what London was for Lenin—"their" place, not a place where social life can nurture the artist or thinker. Hecate County life is a matter of tedious partying, drinking, frustrated lust, snobbery, illness, and despair. The familiar stuff of the suburban novel here has a bizarre spin put on it by an author who portrays his people as haunted by illusions and neuroses. The narrator—himself spooked by friends and by his own personal demons—has moments of lucidity when he retreats to his remote house. But these, too, raise another of the major problems in the Wilson world. Living alone in 1936 in Stamford, Wilson recorded a routine that captures the working life of his Hecate protagonist: "I would go to bed about four—putting myself to sleep with slugs of gin—and get up for lunch about noon."

The book is much more loosely constructed than *Daisy,* actually consisting of a number of short stories bound together by the consciousness of a narrator who recalls scenes from suburban life over a span of some 15 years. The resolutions in the stories, unlike those in *Daisy,* lead the

reader deeper into confusion and ambiguity. After transcending the negativism of the Village in *Daisy,* Wilson leads us into chaotic and demonic
New York and suburban lives—and leaves us there. The stories are peo-
pled by men and women who are severely damaged by insincerity and
illnesses of various kinds. Crafty admen and book club moguls, cracked
lady musicians, and neurotic matrons make a hell for themselves out of
their own dreams and obsessions. The narrator's experience of regeneration in this book is an affair with a Ukrainian dance-hall girl who gives
him gonorrhea.

The first story, "The Man Who Shot Snapping Turtles," is an arresting beginning for a book about social illness. The story is stark and
sparsely written, as dry as some of Wilson's journalistic pieces. Its surface is an odd mixture of allegory and deadly humorous social observation. The protagonist, Asa Stryker, is an eccentric suburban retiree
whose duck pond has been inundated by predatory snapping turtles. He
goes to great lengths to get rid of the ugly predators and protect the
beautiful mallards, only to find the struggle hopeless. The narrator, a
shadowy character here, reminds him to beware of the Manichean
heresy—giving oneself over to the idea that the fate of the world is in
doubt and that the forces of evil can triumph. But Asa—whose Old Testament name expresses his moralistic nature—cannot get his mind off
the conflict. He soon takes the advice of a lax, hard-drinking adman,
Clarence LaTouche, who tells him that there is profit to be had from
changing sides and going into the turtle soup business. Stryker's moral
earnestness is henceforth directed to killing off mallards. Clarence does
the public relations work, and they soon make a fortune. While
Clarence sinks into alcoholism and neglects his interests, Asa manages
the business with the method and rigor he once devoted to killing turtles. It soon dawns on Clarence that he is being cheated, and he, ironically, conceives the notion that Asa will poison him. Almost like a figure
in a medieval exemplum, Clarence falls prey to the homicidal impulse he
has assigned Asa, kills his partner, and is thereafter haunted by guilt and
fear.

Ducks and turtles provide Wilson with an allegorical way of repre-
senting commercial manipulation and the destruction and obsession it
produces. In showing Asa how to get profit from changing the order of
nature, Clarence has also shown him how to get the better of anyone.
Asa's success of course brings him down and is a measure of his illness.
Although the worldly, pragmatic Clarence wins, the price of victory is a
future of dread. As practitioners in two phases of capitalist corruption,

Asa and Clarence emblematize styles of acquisition that troubled Wilson throughout his life. Asa represents the older business ethos, the dour and hard-bitten commercialism that made Pottstown ugly and that Wilson wrote of in his portrait of Engels in Manchester. This is crude exploitation wearing the mask of industriousness and moral uprightness. In the gentlemanly Clarence, Wilson presents the ingratiating, softened, ad agency phase of exploitation. This latter version wins the day in a democratizing society—and kills off the old-fashioned crude approach to moneymaking. In portraying Clarence, Wilson fires realistic and witty volleys against consumer research: the ads for the soup manipulate a public with female sexuality and social status. No outdated patriarch of profit, Clarence uses the latest techniques in selling people what they don't want.

These destructive and obsessed capitalists are followed by artist figures whose lives have their own distortions. In "Ellen Terhune," Wilson makes the pursuit of beauty—an undercurrent in Asa's rage to preserve the ducks—a dominant theme. Here he is continuing to brood on the problem of Rita, the artist wounded by circumstances in early life and afflicted by a neurotic nature. This time, with the experience of *The Wound and the Bow* behind him, Wilson fabricated a much more satisfying story about a young musician. Ellen is the product of a troubled marriage, an unwanted child whose overly large head and strange appearance objectify the wound theme. Like Dickens and others in *The Wound and the Bow,* she is haunted by social conflicts, which in her case include the clash between a genteel mother and a crass father. Ellen's tormented view of herself produces a tormented musical career: she writes two kinds of music—one experimental, obsessive, discordant, and "somewhat mad"; the other highly derivative and flat. The obsession of the story involves her struggle to finish a bizarre-sounding sonata. Meanwhile, the narrator, a sympathetic—indeed, fascinated—neighbor, comes periodically to visit Ellen and catches glimpses of her from the past. Through the device of a time warp, Wilson shows Ellen as a child and a young woman.

Back in the present, Ellen's creation of the sonata has caused her to have a heart attack. The difficult, asocial experiment of course brings to mind the artists of *Axel's Castle,* but this time Wilson has allegorized the problem of the artist who has created something rare and endangering. The narrator's excited response to the strange sonata is mixed with the critical comment of *Axel:* "The piano seemed to be carrying me, like the panic of my dreams, to some bad unintelligible goal." But woven into this presentation is the tragic but affirmative conclusion of *The Wound and the Bow,* that pain is entwined with the triumphal pleasure of art.

"Glimpses of Wilbur Flick" is more about artiness than art. Wilbur, a posturing aesthete who knew the narrator at college, tries to create an identity for himself by living in a Beardsley world of objets d'art. Given the nickname Ducky because of his odd appearance, he at first suggests Bunny Wilson and has caused several commentators to venture the guess that Wilson was dealing with his own escapist, aesthetic side.[7] Although it is true that Wilbur, like Wilson, hated college conventions and loved magic tricks,[8] the portrait is so ridiculous—Wilbur is a pathetic, underendowed, malicious man without redeeming qualities—that it seems hard to believe Wilson deposited much of himself in it.

After being dropped from college, Wilbur embarks on several attempts to make a life for himself. He sets up in New York as a sybarite, complete with a collection of odd animals and a house full of dreadful furniture; after the Crash he lives in Hecate County on a somewhat reduced income, dabbling in aesthetic Catholicism and magic and annoying his neighbors with hideous parties during which he performs musical experiments with Mozart and Gershwin tunes. His conversation is even more offensive than his antics, consisting as it does of fascist remarks about the unemployed and adolescent solutions to the Depression. His drinking and drug taking land him in a sanitarium where he discovers his mission in life—magic and trickery. Thereafter he enjoys a kind of success as a nightclub performer. The narrator gets his last glimpse of Wilbur in the late thirties: he has changed from fascist to leftist; he performs to raise money for the Loyalists in Spain.

Wilson gives us a strong reprise of *The American Earthquake* problem of the empty and fragmented self. Wilbur's Jazz Age fun is as silly, vulgar, and artificial as an evening at the Follies; his taste in art is faddish and pretentious; and he admires the same kind of frivolous experiment that Wilson deplored in the Village during the twenties. When the "big circus" of the twenties is over, his emptiness becomes even more obvious. At the sanitarium the narrator notes that "[t]here seemed to be so little in him when one took him out of his toy palace." Like "Mr. and Mrs. X," the moneyed people dazed by the reversals of the depression, Wilbur has no place in the new world.

In presenting Wilbur's triumph as a magician, Wilson falls into one of his most cynical moods. The leftists themselves, with their talk and dreams of changes, are here shown to have all the venality that we have seen among the opportunistic evangelists in California. Wilbur, who is using his magic act to raise money, is ironically the victim of the Communists who pose as liberals and use him. The 1941 conviction that Wilson expressed about the dictatorship of the proletariat is behind his mordant generalization about leftist politics: Wilbur Flick conceived his circle of radical friends as a "kind of exclusive club which was soon to dominate the world." The story ends with the deadpan cynicism we have seen in *Earthquake:* Wilbur's greatest achievement in his new phase is working for the WPA Theatre Project. He appeared "as a comic embodiment of capitalism who produced a lot of things out of a hat but finally broke down in his act and was denounced as a ridiculous impostor by shrill-voiced young people who represented the workers." When Wilbur loses this job, Wilson remarks that "he couldn't have been more indignant if he had been an expropriated share cropper."

The story is an important marker in Wilson's career as a fiction writer: in its economy and inventiveness, it shows that he is capable of moving beyond rumination and argumentation. Wilbur's actions—as observed by a sensitive narrator—have a reckless and psychologically appropriate quality that doesn't seem to have been worked up to prove a point. Wilson presented the aimlessness of the modern self in *Daisy's* Larry Mickler—the overdramatized nihilist who also likes to get attention—but he has never before described the drifting man of our time with such sharp comment and so little lecturing about man and society.

"The Princess with the Golden Hair" provides even stronger dramatization and explores another kind of failure through a rich use of allegory and seamy naturalism.[9] Sexual life is the ostensible subject matter—a vehicle for revealing a man's values, mistakes, and weaknesses. The plot involves an art historian who moves between two worlds and two women—the world of Hecate County and Imogene, a blonde princess whose sexual spell enchants him, and the world of the Tango Casino on Fourteenth Street, Brooklyn, and Anna, a working-class woman who gives him "actuality." The narrator progresses from a chaotic, almost frenzied pursuit of these women—complete with self-delusions and snobberies—to a rueful recognition of the ways he has duped himself. The story is Wilson's finest piece of fiction—and a distillation of the best in his previous efforts. It gives an honest and credible treatment of sexual life, something that Wilson deserves great credit for at a time when luridness and innuendo would have caused him less trouble with the censors. More generally, Wilson's success comes from his ability to melt ideas into the words and actions and even the furniture of his people.

He blends the representative and the concrete through a skillful and witty use of symbolism and realism. Imogene Loomis, the wife of a WASP business type, lives in a suburban monstrosity of a house built in a pseudo-Elizabethan style reminiscent of Wilson's descriptions of California. The Loomises consume conspicuously, serve pretentious gourmet food, and surround themselves with romantic furnishings. She wears period clothes and cultivates cocktail conversation that is cutesy-erotic; the narrator falls for her as they exchange mock-Arthurian remarks about love. Wilson coarsens the texture of his story with such tripe not only to present a vision of suburban life but also to lead us into the larger problem of fantasies and confusions. The narrator embarks on a frustrating seduction campaign—in quest of a kinky ideal woman. Imogene, besides being luxurious and coy, is afflicted with a strange back problem. (Rita's neurosis and Ellen's problems have here been related to sexual fascination rather than artistic power.) The narrator sees her back brace—a fetishistic turn-on for him—only after his two-year pursuit. Their lovemaking is unsatisfactory ("she did it all for herself"), even though she is passionate and beautiful and he is a veritable hero from a pornographic novel. Behind the dissatisfaction is the spooky, neurotic world of the Loomises: she indulges herself in wild daydreaming about living in Italian villas, uses her husband to support her fantasies, and takes advantage of her ailment—which, it turns out, is a psychosomatic wound. Enchanted for a time by Imogene's perversity—which is a cheap variation of the exotic experience and isolation in *Axel's Castle*—the narrator awakens to the fact that he has played the part of the contemporary knight-errant in pursuit of a diseased witchy ideal.

The scenes with Imogene are rendered in a prose that is at once rhapsodic and ironic. Together the lovers create romantic scenarios for themselves while drinking in suburban roadhouses. The narrator alternates between dour resignation and embroidered dreams about living in a castle in Ireland:

> I suddenly found myself cloyed with this idyl of gay Irish hunting and rosy-cheeked old Irish servants, and I insisted that the things she was having us do were far too expensive for us, that my income was very much smaller than Ralph's. . . . I saw myself getting muzzy over Prohibition cocktails, which had been served in depressing teacups, amid the hunting prints of the Hecate County roadhouse—these had bested the south of Ireland dream-fugue—talking idiotic might-have-beens with the wife of an advertising man.

The baroque endearments that the lovers exchange are sometimes punctuated by Wilson's odd, jarring sense of humor. "Now that you've had me," Imogene remarks, "you don't care whether I have any soda in my drinks!" And the very preposterousness of Imogene's sentiments and manners—combining atrocious pseudoculture, superficial genteel consideration, and wide-eyed girlishness—provide an ironically comic commentary on the upper class. Part of the irony, of course, is how our sexually overheated narrator is taken in by Imogene's witchiness. In "the subsoil" of his mind, he has always desired "the American beauty"—and Wilson goes so far as to have his protagonist fall not only for Imogene but also for the picture of a cigarette-smoking girl on a magazine cover, "a lovely girl, photographed from life, with teasing and sincere brown eyes, posing against the background of a golden tobacco leaf and dressed in a clarion red hat that seemed a blast of blood-shaking emotion."

As in Wilson's journals *The Thirties,* there is some coldness in the protagonist's attitude toward women. Most of it can be accounted to the portrait of a seducer that Wilson is drawing, but some of his candid reactions are tainted by Wilson's besetting problem with human involvement and feeling. Diana Trilling finds the protagonist's decisive attitude after he discovers Imogene's neurosis to be disturbing: once he discovers that she is emotionally disturbed, he begins to think of good times and other women.[10] The ending of the relationship—"she and I, for all our romancings, could never have a world in common"—while believable enough, seems to be no surprise and makes us wonder why the protagonist, with his enlightened social views and his keen aesthetic sense, continued to pursue this woman. Of course, lust is the answer—but when desire is damaged by an exceptionally neurotic enchantress, it's time to philosophize.

Yet lust does not necessarily lead to the barren resolution of the Imogene relationship. Paradoxically the same feelings can lead him to some knowledge and a kind of love. While pursuing Imogene, he finds some dry spots in his life and takes up with Anna Lenihan, a woman whose nature is unencumbered by the baggage of tour-guide fantasies. This Brooklyn woman suffers from her social situation and is also diseased, but she is not the sly carrier of poisonous enchantment. A member of the underclass rather than a princess, she puts the narrator in touch with actualities, which he, in turn, twists out of shape.

Wilson's treatment of the relationship includes the progress of the narrator from a naive kind of romantic Marxism to a deeply saddened, humanistic understanding that includes sympathy, love, and a keen sense of life's limits. The narrator begins with a head full of ideologies; he hangs around Fourteenth Street "making a little sociological survey"—looking at working-class girls. During this period he has also come to reject Clive Bell's aesthetic theories, which "made art represent a reality independent of life." The abstractions that Bell admired in art are also rejected by a socially aware narrator who would "want to leave explicit in any painting of Anna some evidence of her tarnished prettiness."

The theorizing narrator soon is consumed with the complications of real life—including Anna's bloomers and the details of her anatomy. Thus "——ing in the afternoon" becomes a major occupation, but soon, with "appetite" so satisfactorily "increased," this rather cool experimenter is upset by an obstacle in his proletarian idyll. The matured and deepened narrator records the pettiness and distrust he felt when he discovered that Anna had infected him. He also records his distanced, naive way of dealing with the lower classes: they are victims of class injustice rather than ordinary people whom one treats as equals. The manner in which the protagonist swathes his feelings for a woman in political rhetoric is the major irony here: "I felt that Karl Marx and Anna had given me the right to be bitter." Or "But the world of Anna was the real world, the base on which everything rested." The "world of Anna," regrettably, is just another way of reducing the reality of Anna to some easily graspable formula.

The protagonist's sounder recognitions come after he has discovered that the Imogene ideal is so much "adolescent mooning." After this point sees something ugly about his relations with Anna. Since he has been victimized and frustrated by Imogene, he has taken out his aggressions on someone weaker, and done so with romantic Marxist phrases on his lips. Anna has been a battered wife, a struggling mother, and a member of a sordid household. What better person to receive an ideologue's goodwill? The culmination of her troubles—a serious gynecological operation—causes the narrator to take a look at his own motives. Was he getting pleasure from seeing her,

> as the wretched butt of the brutality of the capitalist system?—from having her, by reason of her poverty, of her humility, of her gratitude toward me, at the same sort of insuperable disadvantage as that at which Imogene had for so long held me? And now was I not really gloating, under pretense of pity and fear, over, virtually, her disembowelment?

Such a recognition should be compared to Blake's "Pity would be no more, / If we did not make somebody Poor."

But just as Wilson shows his protagonist discovering his own coldness and ugliness, he throws us another ironic curve. True to human weakness rather than to a schematic plot or a Marxist line, Wilson shows his persona falling back into his old suspicions about the lower classes: Anna, he decides, is not honest. Soon he is "rescued by a deus ex machina in the shape of my old girl, Jo Gates."

The story is resolved as the narrator returns to the cocktail set in Hecate County. He knows what he has lost—the actuality, "the true sanction for life" given by Anna. For a while his two best instincts had broken down the barriers between Hecate and the larger world. Desire and a passion for art had "brought me to her through the prison of the social compartments, across the clutter of the economic mess." The second passion is what the narrator emphasizes, but the paradox of the story is that desire drove him to seek satisfaction and that Anna, a good and gentle woman, humanized his desire. While his Marxist rhetoric was as false and corrupt as his fairy-tale fabrications with Imogene, art and desire have given a kind of dignity to his years of experience. But having approached the headquarters of humanity in his sometimes tender feelings for Anna, he is drawn back to Hecate by his own prejudices and by the force of circumstances.

The brouhaha over the sex in this story is of course hard to understand in a world where soft-core pornographic novels set in suburbia have become a popular commodity.[11] Wilson, however, while he was the founding father of the suburban shocker, never engages in the wild and serious fantasies of pornographers. Deadly ironic most of the time, he is keenly aware of his protagonist's shortcomings—even if they resemble his own. Raymond Chandler, perhaps the liveliest commentator on Wilson's use of sexuality, has missed some of this irony in criticizing Wilson for making "fornication as dull as a railroad time table."[12] While "indecent enough," Wilson's book is "without passion, like a phallus made of dough." The fact is, however, that Chandler has ignored the developmental aspect of this story. At times Wilson's rather mechanical narrator records his adventures in a flat, naturalistic style, but other passages are filled with emotion, and they show a protagonist approaching a new world of feeling. The idea of feeling and paralysis of feeling that informs "The Princess" was well understood by Robert Warshow, one of the few critics who saw the commanding intellectual vision of the book. He observed that Wilson's ugly scenes and blurring of fantasy and reality were ways a writer had of creating "a valid response" to modern life. There is no possible new world of feeling in the last two stories of *Memoirs of Hecate County*. The episodes have a certain stale, contrived quality, despite a few good scenes. Concerned with American desolation, they often seem mired in it. Wilson has fallen prey to what Yvor Winters called "the fallacy of imitative form"—following chaotic reality too closely.[13]

"The Milhollands and Their Damned Soul" is an overburdened story about the rise of American literary commercialism. The Milholland brothers—one a former second-rate professor, the other a Midwestern rube—have propelled themselves into a series of big-time book club and magazine enterprises directed to middlebrows with a thirst for culture and novelty. Their success is based on having passed off their failures on the sad sack Flagler Haynes, a publisher who takes their risks, does their dirty work, acts as a stalking horse for their ideas, and even takes discarded mistresses. Through a compact with the devil, the brothers have unloaded all their misfortunes. The poorly sustained suspense of this story is involved with the threat that the Old One will come to collect. About all that happens in this regard is that the naive brother kills himself over a scandal: the magazine was running a personals page for its kinkier readers. The sharper brother lives to eulogize the poor fool and soon goes into TV and schlock novels. While lives are ground down by pseudoculture, Milholland and his smart nephew Spike enter the electronic age.

This loose allegory of intellectual corruption is given color by Wilson's humorous gargoyles and arabesques. The elaboration is sometimes as clever as "Wilbur Flick" and "Snapping Turtles" and has a bearing on Wilson's deepest concerns. The attack on the selling of culture—what Irving Howe has analyzed as contemporary society's capacity for turning ideas into watered-down commodities[14]—is occasionally devastating. Spike, a onetime thirties radical student, becomes a TV personality and "barker for Parnassus." His job is to publicize a hideous *Gone with the Wind*–type novel written by his uncle's cohorts. The book is a distillation of commercialism, with soft-core porn, sentimentality, exploitation of sappy ideas about the nativist experience, and a bit of history. Si Banks, a poor drudge enlisted for this, writes a passage about "Nancy Gaylord" as the mother of Walt Whitman's illegitimate child: "He meets her at the Mardi Gras and lays her on a cotton bale."

Hecate County ends in the moral doldrums with "Mr. and Mrs. Blackburn at Home," a tedious story that nevertheless has some memorable scenes and significant ruminations. The Blackburns are sinister and very rich members of the cocktail set, and Wilson contrives a demonic set of characteristics for Ed Blackburn, including a shifty manner, a delight in Western civilization's decline, and three gold front teeth. Such stuff is meant to direct us into the general atmosphere of decadence. With these people—and guests like the vulgar Hollywood writer Reggie da Luze— the narrator sinks back into his worst self: he uses the gorilla-like approach to lovemaking to take revenge on Jo Gates for looking at another man. In an especially brutal episode he tells us that "my club seemed to burn and exult in liberation." Soon thereafter he leaves the party where he abused Jo in an upstairs bedroom and returns to his own house, "a lodge that was almost like a castle," where he can commune with his books and his "solitary self." Once again Axel is used as a counter, this time with tremendous irony.

Although his book on nineteenth-century art is finished, the narrator is something of a wreck intellectually as well as socially. He goes off to the West with Jo, only to find Hecate County out there waiting for him. With damaged spirit, he looks out, "divided by a pane of glass" from "the new world which seemed to be just at hand." The wonder and yearning at the end of *The Great Gatsby*—Wilson's friend's novel about the idea of American civilization—is transformed by Wilson into boredom and worse: "I had packed bad nights with my baggage."

As an ending, this leaves us in a disintegrating world.

Chapter Six
From the Civil War to the MLA

After writing about the earthquake and the jitters of the early thirties, Wilson created a vision of order and hope by using the stories of revolutionary socialists in *To the Finland Station;* but no sooner did he create this vision than his own faith in Marxism began to be eroded by the growth of the Soviet state. The idea of a headquarters of humanity located in a particular country was damaged by the realities of politics—by the Moscow Trials and by the Hitler-Stalin Pact of 1939. Wilson's dreams about autonomy and human liberation in Russia were dissolved by the end of the thirties.[1] By the forties he had returned to the skepticism and discontent that he started out with as a young journalist; in Sherman Paul's words, Wilson found that the Finland Station opened out on Hecate County—and also on the ravaged and corrupt Europe that he reported on in *Europe Without Baedeker.*

What came next in Wilson's career as an observer of the contemporary scene was at once predictable in attitude and remarkable in range and analysis. Certainly Wilson presents the landscape of the fifties and sixties as dominated by social and political tyranny, intellectual shrinkage, and burnout. Irving Howe has characterized an aspect of Wilson's attitude as "a radicalism of nausea,"[2] a generalized disgust with the working of American and European civilization. If Wilson had only such an attitude to offer, his writing would hardly be important. But his best new political-literary exploration, *Patriotic Gore,* and some lesser works such as *Apologies to the Iroquois* and *The Cold War and the Income Tax* are exciting because of the author's command of vast bodies of knowledge, his disquieting insights and applications of his research, and his ability to leave his readers—those who stayed with him after the Second World War—with a sense that there is a pattern in our lives as citizens of a modern state, one that needs the tracing out of a master critic. Much of Wilson's postwar energy was devoted to the analysis of the Western power drive—where it came from, the forms it takes, what we can do about it.

Throughout the fifties and sixties Wilson worked on an awesome assembling of acts of oppression and power in his own country: minds manacled by ideologies and patriotic sentiments, writers creating in an environment of propaganda and intimidation, minority groups swindled by the government, taxpayers bamboozled and charged for bombs, small countries at the mercy of the American empire, American literature dominated by organized professional scholars. The American power drive—whether the impulse to create a "more perfect Union" or the desire to dominate the study of literature with definitive, scholarly editions of classic works—was part of Wilson's reportorial beat during the years after World War II. Once he had studied the impotence of capitalists and the inertia of leaders in the thirties; now he undertook to analyze the brute force of the world's most successful power unit. He used literary criticism, history, drama, straight reporting, and polemics to explore his own sense of outrage.

Patriotic Gore, a book about the Civil War and its baleful consequences for our social, political, and intellectual life, is Wilson's most significant expression of his ideas about American power. The project is one of Wilson's most impressive enterprises. Proportioned like *To the Finland Station*—but indeed much larger—the book is subtitled "Studies in the Literature of the Civil War." It surveys and analyzes the impact of the war and its issues on writers, thinkers, and public figures—some of great merit and continuing relevance, some whose work is tedious and of historical interest only. The oddity of the book can be seen in its choices and its relentlessness: everybody is here who felt deeply about the war, but major figures like Walt Whitman are often given brief treatment as Wilson plows through the life and works of a minor writer such as John William De Forest. Wilson gives us what H. L. Mencken once referred to as "vast steppes and pampas" of prose; the highlighting technique of *To the Finland Station,* with its strategy of public-private presentation of careers, here is displaced by a less selective and dramatic method. In evoking the attitudes of a forgotten Civil War figure, Wilson often overburdens his chapters with detail and employs huge blocks of quoted matter to convey his ideas.

The book's genesis can be traced to 1923 when Wilson's father, a great admirer of Lincoln, died. Kenneth Lynn describes clearly how Wilson's interests were sparked:

> The senior Wilson admired Lincoln enormously . . . and was fond of giving a speech called "Lincoln the Great Commoner." His son automatically made a point of knowing as little about Lincoln as possible, and considered his father's interest in the subject to be a pose which "verged upon demagoguery." For while the elder Wilson wished to serve the com-

mon people, he was no commoner himself, and he lacked the common touch; he dealt with political crowds, as well as the clients who came to his office, *de haut en bas.* Only after his father's death did the author of *Patriotic Gore* come to understand his parent's kinship with Lincoln. For he now read Herndon's life of Lincoln, which his father had always told him was the least sentimental of the biographies. and at last realized that here was "a great lawyer who was deeply neurotic, who had to struggle with great spells of depression, and who . . . had managed, in spite of his handicap, to bring through his own nightmares and the crisis of society— somewhat battered—the American Republic."[3]

It seems that Wilson's interest proceeded in part from reading about a demystified Lincoln, a stern and troubled figure unlike the log-cabin saint of the popular imagination. Curiosity about his father's austere achievements—about how men overcome circumstances and about how their triumph may be a form of tyranny—also played its part.

But along with these points of engagement for a mind like Wilson's, two other circumstances brought the study into being: Wilson's continuing fascination with wounds and his distress about the growth of the American empire. *Patriotic Gore*—the title itself directs us back to *The Wound and the Bow;* the injury and the weapon of the 1941 book are now conflated into a new image taken from the song "Maryland! My Maryland!"—the weapon of ideology (patriotic feeling) stained with blood. The central idea that informs Wilson's book is an adaptation of his belief that great ideas and achievements have their origins in disease and suffering. The achievement in the case of *Patriotic Gore* is seen in two ways: in a literary sense, it is the illness that writers shed and employ in their books; in a political sense, it is Lincoln's preservation of the Union. For Wilson the disease of the Civil War is the seething blood lust, greed, and territorial ambition of the North and South that have been masked by moral sentiments and rhetoric. This new adaptation has, in a sense, destroyed the grandeur and heroism of *The Wound and the Bow* idea by viewing political order and a great deal of literary achievement— whether Ulysses S. Grant's imperturbable prose style or Oliver Wendell Holmes's stoical, duty-bound "Soldier's Faith" or Ambrose Bierce's death-obsessed writings—as responses to the pressures of dictators such as (you guessed it) Abraham Lincoln. Although this vision was shaped over a long period, it emerged most clearly in Wilson's letters from the 1950s in which he calls America "an expanding power unit" and refers to American idealism as "eyewash." The "bureaucratic and monolithic" country of the post–World War II period caused Wilson to look back a hundred years for the origins of our power drive.

In a 1947 review, "Van Wyck Brooks on the Civil War," Wilson foreshadowed his major concerns. The war "left the American republican idealism in a wretched and demoralized state, dislocating the points of view of writers, Northern and Southern alike, whose training had prepared them for a different kind of world from that with which they were later confronted." The idea of democratic civilization was badly damaged for both fine and ordinary minds, and the war ushered in a new era of ruthless business competition—the period of Wilson's father's young manhood—when a "general shrinking and chill" pervaded the national life. Wilson speaks of the period as "the moment of bankruptcies and wounds, of miscarriages, distortions, frustrations."

Such feelings took a more definite shape as Wilson began to write about his approaches to his new project. Early on, he said he was writing something like *To the Finland Station;* his idea was "to excavate a period" and "to set our values straight."[4] But, unlike *To the Finland Station,* the new book was about "a taboo subject"—the brutality behind our national pieties. By the eve of completion, Wilson was working on a polemical introduction that expressed his latest philosophy of history. In trying to "get behind politics," he was urging on his readers a new and alarming theory of causation: man at war was a devouring sea slug who differed from the beasts only in his ability to rationalize. Part Marxist probing into the material realities behind historical conflicts, part homemade rather than scholarly anthropology and zoology, this view of events represents a real change in Wilson's philosophy of history. While some critics have found the introduction reductive and unconnected to the "literature of the Civil War," the fact remains that it is thematically related to his portraits of people damaged and driven by war.[5]

If we place the openings of *To the Finland Station* and *Patriotic Gore* side by side, we see the distance Wilson has travelled. The first book is about circumstances that shape men who in turn learn to reshape their world. *Finland Station,* like the other works of the thirties, is essentially about freedom, the progress toward an ideal; it sees men as making history, but not just as they choose. *Patriotic Gore,* however, places emphasis on what men have not chosen: overmastering lusts and instincts, confusions, superstitions, mysticism, and national myths that paralyze critical thought. Although it has its heroes, it is essentially about victims.

Wilson pursues three consequences of the Civil War: the pattern of centralization in our national life, the impact of the war on writing styles, and the myths and spiritual flights of men as they seek to explain their attraction to power. In developing the first idea he exhibits his characteristic tendency to draw controversial comparisons. He compares Lincoln, Lenin, and Bismarck as national unifiers; each "became an uncompromising dictator, and each was succeeded by agencies which continued to exercise this power and to manipulate the people he had been unifying in a stupid, despotic and unscrupulous fashion." In order to pursue this aspect of the argument, Wilson employs the reasoning and testimony of a variety of writers who have found the idea of the nation-state repellent. Wilson the freethinker and anti-ideologue ranges over huge bodies of writing—some produced by good and intelligent men, some produced by fanatics—in pursuit of sentiments that resemble his own.

George Fitzhugh, author of *Sociology for the South,* provides Wilson with the opportunity to air his own disdain for American nationalism. Wilson describes Fitzhugh's anti-laissez-faire position—that of the southerner defending his own region against the unifying drive and commercialism of the North. Fitzhugh advances the notion that the Declaration of Independence and the Constitution are nonsense: the "consent of the governed" is hypocrisy in a country of northern plutocrats who dominate the weak. The chapter on Fitzhugh is at once powerful and complicated. It hits hard at big money and is informed by the moral conscience that made *The American Earthquake* an important critique of our society, but it is laced with skepticism and irony as Wilson shows us that Fitzhugh, the enemy of capitalism, is at the same time a defender of slavery. Wilson's purpose appears to be to expose moral pretense: he leads the reader into doubt and distrust—even of people who attack northern money. The irony of this is compounded when Wilson reminds us that Fitzhugh the fanatic coined the phrase "house divided" to describe his protest against the anarchy and chaos of northern-style economic and social freedom; Lincoln, as it were, used an abhorrent bigot as an intellectual source. Showing the entangled nature of our so-called moral life is a characteristic Wilson ploy. Even the nobler impulses of his heroes in *To the Finland Station* have been connected with brutality; in *Patriotic Gore* he makes the connections more frequently and emphasizes their centrality. Even sound, rational ideas—such as distrust of the Union's power—issue from minds filled with hatred and rage.

Another anti-Union writer, Alexander H. Stephens, the vice president of the Confederacy, wins admiration, even though Wilson must admit that Stephens's voice in *A Constitutional View of the Late War between the States* is that of a "merciless old ideologue." Stephens, a sickly scholar who took up the cause of rationalizing states' rights and demolishing the intellectual position of Lincoln, becomes a kind of tainted hero as he defends the individual against the "pack" and the Lincolnian idea of our national "destiny." For his protest against the Union, which is preserved in a huge "mausoleum" of a book, the frail Stephens earns this memorial sentence: "It was as if he had shrunk to pure principle, abstract, incandescent, indestructible." Needless to say, Wilson's critics among the liberals have balked at such reverence for an obvious southern apologist. While they are quite right to be startled by Wilson's praise, they have not paused to evaluate his overall design in exploring power and have neglected the ironic tincture of many portraits in the book. With Lincoln in the grip of destiny, with abolitionists hearing the voice of God, with "The Battle Hymn of the Republic" being directed from beyond, with complex contemporaries like Henry James standing on the sidelines rather than taking part in the struggle of ideas, any voice of resistance that criticizes the monolithic state commands attention.

The literary styles of the period are also a reflection of the ways writers submitted to or attempted to master the drive for national unification. Wilson's pages on romanticism, hard-edged plainness, and complex ambiguity show how the writer's relationship to his society's upheaval determines his way of using language and sometimes determines his attitude toward life itself. Wilson uses a Marxist analysis of literature and life as he shows the complex reciprocity between style and social conflicts.[6] In writing about Sir Walter Scott and the ways he contributed to the formation of a florid, antebellum romanticism, Wilson argues that the style is a congealing of southern values and an instrument for furthering illusions about southern moral superiority and graciousness. Wilson half humorously employs Mark Twain's idea that the influence of Scott was "in great measure responsible for the war." Twain had described Scott as setting "the world in love with dreams and phantasms; with decayed and swinish forms of religion; with decayed and degraded forms of government; with the silliness and emptiness, sham grandeurs, sham gauds, and sham chivalries of a brainless and worthless long-vanished society." Wilson follows this blustery attack on neo-medievalism with a solid analysis of the ways in which writers have fed on fantasies and thereby ruined their talents. Sidney Lanier, a writer whom Wilson commends for his devotion to literature, was overwhelmed and intellectually paralyzed by dreamy romanticism. Thomas

Page, one of the third-rate writers on whom Wilson lavishes analysis, did worse things with the heritage of Scott. A post–Civil War southerner pandering to northerners who wanted to read about the "gracious life" of the Old South, Page invented the stereotypes of "Old Massa" and "Meh Lady"—the benevolent plantation owners who would reappear in countless trashy novels. Wilson sets up his presentation of Page to tell us more than this, however. The Scott legacy, as it appears in the works of Page, contributes to a dangerous anesthetizing of perception: the torment of the southerner is reduced to something cozy and sentimental. Wilson shows how the southern writer of Page's sort harms his fellow southerners by adorning their illusions: "Animosities must be forgotten; the old issues must be put to sleep with the chloroform of magazine prose."

The forging of the modern plain style—what Wilson calls "the language of responsibility"—poses an even greater problem for the analyst of the Civil War. Ulysses S. Grant and other literary soldiers "chastened" prose style as they wrote under the pressures of the war and with the need for directness and lucidity in their communication with ordinary readers. Beginning with Grant, an unlikely choice for a discussion of literary style, Wilson treats the question of America's literary and intellectual future. The prosaic tone of Grant's *Memoirs*—the imperturbability, coolness, and lack of surface drama—has its values and limitations. Wilson's best, most ambivalent response comes into play. In one sense the plain style is a great leap forward in American writing: "We shall be caught here in no leatherstocking thicket; we shall be bound by no apocalyptic imagery; we shall not have to plod against the clotting of a too long pent-up introspection." In expressing his attraction to the American plain style—the prose of Mark Twain, Hemingway, and his own books—Wilson also expresses his reservations about writers who elaborate on their subjects in an odd manner. He assails stylistically obscure writers like Fenimore Cooper just as he forthrightly took Valéry and Joyce to task in *Axel's Castle*.

But once these feelings are expressed, Wilson qualifies them—and indeed complicates his own position about good style—by exploring the deadly implications of the new chastened style. He criticizes what he is most attracted to as he analyzes correctness, plainness, and brevity. One of Wilson's finest stretches of criticism in the book concerns Ambrose Bierce, a writer whose limitations can be seen in his "marble correctitude." Wilson's approach is reminiscent of "Uncomfortable Casanova" in *The Wound and the Bow:* he shows that Bierce's career was warped by

Calvinism, by neglect in youth, and by the routine spectacle of death in the Civil War. Wilson argues that the damaged author was capable of creating only one character: "Death" crowds out all human concerns and all human sympathy; Bierce's writings are precise, clear, and orderly—almost military—communications about how people get killed. Wilson concludes that this hard-edged prose is a "mask for a certain vulgarity of mind and feeling." It suggests that some "short circuit had blown out an emotional fuse." But the disease in question—Bierce's failure to respond sympathetically despite his ability to write elegantly—is traced back to the conditions of the war. The appearance of the plain style—at once a relief from the adornment of the romantic style and an experiment in severity—is a significant event in national letters. Wilson called the plain style of Grant's *Memoirs* "part of that vision of the Civil War that Lincoln imposed on the nation." Wilson is exploring what he considers our national numbness and the ways in which correct and authoritative authors have created an empire of communication that comes down to us in the imperturbability of the military order and the bureaucratic memorandum.

Wilson contrasts the new "language of responsibility" with the ambiguous responses of Henry James, a young man who was physically unfit for military service. Even the noncombatant is profoundly affected by the fact of the Civil War, however. Wilson undertakes to describe a way in which ambiguous response to the American upheaval contributed to the formation of a unique style. In dealing with James, Wilson argues that the "effect of the war may be traced in opposite qualities—ambiguity, prolixity, irony—that reflect a kind of lack of self-confidence, a diffidence and a mechanism of self-defense." Wilson's James is at once detached from the war his brothers fought in and involved with it in a peculiar fashion. While James does not write about the war in his fiction, he describes in a late memoir a "comprehensive ache" that seemed to pervade society and his own injured being. Wilson maintains that James never forgot the trauma of being left out. His reading of the famous ghost story "The Jolly Corner" sees James as impressed and ultimately horrified by a would-be self in the form of an apparition—a figure who was powerful and menacing, and had been wounded in the war. Recoiling from this image of the new American as victorious warrior, James is nevertheless fascinated by the idea of American conquest. Wilson shows Henry James, a "poor worm of peace and quiet," yearning for literary campaigns and conquest and thinking about early twentieth-century life in terms of the Civil War.

This portrait of James is clearly informed by the ideas that Wilson used in portraying Dickens, and yet it strives to make a larger generalization about the relation of trauma to style. Wilson views James as building a new and unique empire of his own—not that of involvement and force, but a strange, impressionistic empire of style forged in response to his own feelings about power. Once again Wilson identifies the negative features of the style—as he has done with Bierce—while taking in the mastery that it achieves. Once again his emphasis falls on the distance from the actuality of the world, a distance seen in the works of Bierce and the romanticists as well. This time, however, there is a great monument, not the death's-head of Bierce or the meretricious stereotyping of Page. While the "weaving and swathing" of James's language gets "further and further away from the direct presentation of the actual world"—the world that Wilson was trying to come in contact with in the major books of his career—that very elaboration "makes possible a poetic richness," a style comparable with that of the symbolists. Here James's empire is identified and critically examined, and indeed traced to its foundations, as Axel's poets were related to their forebears. Psychological, aesthetic, and historical approaches are brought to bear as Wilson evaluates a style formed under the pressure of an American crisis.

While the analysis of prose style is one way Wilson has of describing American destiny since the Civil War, the scrutiny of spiritual ideals leads him to his most pessimistic conclusions about the power drive. Working as an intellectual historian and literary critic, Wilson shows how people of integrity as well as scoundrels and fanatics identified their ideas about the war with God's will. The portrait of Lincoln is one of Wilson's finest studies of intellectual change, a delicately responsive tracing of how an Illinois freethinker became a prophet who "crushed opposition and sent thousands of men to their deaths" in the name of the mystical Union. As a literary critic Wilson shows the emergence of the sermon form in Lincoln's speeches. As a historian experienced in the analysis of the ways in which political necessities give shape to ideas, he shows how Lincoln found it expedient to invoke the Lord of Hosts and how he came to see the issues of the Civil War "in a light more and more religious, in more and more Scriptural terms, under a more and more apocalyptic aspect. The vision had imposed itself." Combining a sense of awe and skepticism in his response to one man's conscience, Wilson sweeps away sentimental notions about Lincoln ("the cruellest thing that has happened to Lincoln since he was shot by Booth has been to fall into the hands of Carl Sandburg") and replaces them with the severe grandeur of "the epic that Lincoln directed and lived and wrote." Other spirit-driven figures are treated with less respect. Julia Ward Howe, who wrote the words of "The Battle Hymn of the Republic," is presented in an insinuating portrait, the major idea of which is to show how the freight of the Puritan past was unloaded onto a favorite tune. Wilson the literary detective traces the origin of the lyrics both to the Old Testament and to a song of the English Civil War. We watch as the source of the feelings comes clear: "In this case, the cause of the North was associated by Julia Ward Howe not merely with God's punishments of the enemies of Israel but also with the victory over the Royalists and Papists of Ireton's Cromwellian army." His purpose is to show how Calvinist doctrine finds its way into our most patriotic and emotional outpourings.

His portraits of outright fanatics constitute the far end of the religious-mystical continuum. Wilson of course shows disdain for his subjects, yet he holds our interest—and makes his project into a kind of public service—by studying the growth of diseased ideals. One of the most disturbing portraits of American illness is that of Hinton Helper, a southerner with a grudge against the plantation owners. He first attacked slavery as an unprofitable institution and later turned his resentment against the blacks themselves. At first Wilson writes about the "stream of exhilarating invective whose directness and outspokenness seem bracing after the sophistries of southern apologetics." But later we are shown the workings of a mind that wanted to "write the Negro out of America." In this chapter Wilson makes a major contribution to the understanding of American racism. Wilson analyzes a chapter in Helper's book called "Black: A Thing of Ugliness, Disease." In the course of evaluating Helper's bizarre ideas about physiological inferiority and the horror of blackness, Wilson leads us into a terrifying moral universe—and not merely to watch the spectacle of moral confusion. He purposely employs a phrase from his Lincoln portrait that not only echoes in our minds but creates a grim consonance between a fanatic and a great president: Helper, he tells us, had "a certain power of imposing himself" and Lincoln's vision "had imposed itself."

The clarification of the ways in which famous men and now forgotten ones like Helper imposed their visions on the American scene is Wilson's major achievement in *Patriotic Gore*. The book's sweep, its depth of analysis, its naturalistic approach to high-flown sentiments make it one of his most ambitious works.[7] As he marches through the Civil War landscape, pointing out the ways in which writers were overwhelmed by visions and prejudices, he shows great fortitude and moral balance. Who else has so brilliantly resuscitated so many second-rate figures, thrown such an odd light on major ones, and imbued his subjects with such significance? What other American critic has done so thorough a job of warning us about how war shapes consciousness?

Descending from one of Wilson's most ambitious assaults on America to his more modest undertakings is bound to produce a dizzying effect. He criticized other facets of the American power drive but never again achieved the grandeur of his Civil War approach. For years he was in the habit of depositing in his plays the anger he felt about the drift of our culture. One of these plays, *The Little Blue Light,* is an interesting culmination of his own anxieties about America. In it he reaches a highwater mark of resentment and fear as he presents a fantastic vision of what the power drive is likely to mean in the future. Written in the late forties and produced at the ANTA theater in New York in 1951, the play is a less controlled, indeed almost hysterical presentation of the theme of centralization—the subject that he would explore with such mastery in *Patriotic Gore.*

The plot of *The Little Blue Light*—at once preposterous and predictive of movie and television scripts about strange phenomena—concerns an old-fashioned crusading magazine editor, Frank Brock; his restive, destructive wife, Judith; a haunted writer of bizarre fantasies named Gandersheim; and the forces of evil in the modern world—a syndicate led by a gangster named Teniakis. The action—much like an episode of Rod Serling's *The Twilight Zone*—takes place in the "not-so-remote future" as Gandersheim, the Brocks' landlord, returns from a war-ravaged Europe and goes to work for Brock as a writer. "Gandy," an old "St. Matthews [read Hill School] man," is troubled by the puritanical character of his upbringing and fascinated by his own creations, especially one Shidnats Slyme, a nonhuman "force that blights and kills." Within the structure of the play, Gandersheim represents the power and vision of the writer whose seemingly wild fantasies are intimations of a new and terrifying reality. As the action unfolds, his writing becomes a representation of what is happening in America.

Frank Brock has been battling various pressure groups, notably "the Peters" (read the Roman Catholic Church). Recently one of the Peters has been killed, and suspicion has fallen on one of Brock's employees. The play traces the Peter's violent death to another power unit, the Teniakis Bureau, a benevolent association run by a rich Greek. This Mafia-like operation finds jobs for people and helps the community while infiltrating legitimate business and intimidating the press. It liquidates its opponents by using a little blue light that kills them when they register anger, hatred, or other intense emotions. By the end of the play, Judith has turned on her husband, gone over to the syndicate side, and—in one of the clumsiest endings in American theater history—set off the little blue light of hate.

Despite the hokey plot making, the play contains a core of intellectual seriousness and moral fervor that should not be dismissed from a view of Wilson the social critic. Wilson is disturbed by "the demiurge that is running amuck, devouring civilization"; "call it the Second Coming, like Yeats, with a wild beast instead of a savior—call him Shidnats Slyme, the Monster God." The Teniakis Bureau helps the needy, rewards the servile, and generally enjoys the favor of docile citizens. When a man of intellectual curiosity and vision comes along—Frank Brock is as feisty and forthright as Wilson in denouncing corruption—he is the perfect object on which to direct the little blue light. Wilson, in turn, has directed the light of melodrama and fantasy on his own enemies—strong lobbies, monopolists, and others who offer their fellow citizens tyranny and call it progress and humanitarianism. The play adumbrates, in its crude way, the powerful indictments of *Patriotic Gore*.

Beyond this attack on the agencies that dominate Americans and hedge them in, the play offers a warning and a moral prescription. Throughout the course of the action, a mysterious old gardener employed by the Brocks hovers around the central characters and makes cryptic remarks about them: this rather heavy-handed commentator turns out to be the Wandering Jew, a figure of legend who here appears in his latest guise. Wilson uses this outlaw, "who mocked at our prophet Christ, who told him to walk faster as he carried the cross and who therefore was sentenced to wander till Christ should return again," as the bearer of a tradition older than Christianity—"the conscience, the courage, the insight by which men of a chosen race asserted their superior authority." The Wandering Jew is present at the last scene in the play. It is Christmas Eve and the Brocks, imaginative and intelligent people, destroy themselves and fall into the net of their enemies through their own bad conscience and contentiousness. The gardener-commentator asks, "Is the star of Bethlehem setting?" A resounding "No" comes next as the Wandering Jew resolves to continue giving witness to the "Light"—God's Light—"at some man's side!" This is the latest echo of the resolve in "A Preface to Persius"—the humanist's commitment to battle the darkness and the "alien shapes" of modern civilization. Regrettably this moment of moral grandeur is incredibly stagey and has been prepared for an audience that has already been made to despair by seeing the spectacle of Wilson's trapped people. The drama critic Harold Clurman responded to the play's impact by commenting that Wilson throws the little blue light of despair on us.[8] Dramatic affirmation in the final scene is not enough to overthrow the sense that intelligence and public spirit are weaker forces in the modern world than are power lust and guile.

After setting up this nightmare vision of American entrapment, Wilson had the strange, poetically appropriate misfortune to become the victim of a power unit—not the Mafia, but "that son of a bitch Uncle Sam." In *The Cold War and the Income Tax* he describes his own failure to file income tax returns between 1946 and 1955. As a writer with a small income and no steady job, he simply neglected to file. The "delinquent"—at first a confused man rather than a principled protester—was soon "in the hands of the IRS." There were huge fines, hearings, investigations of his personal life, and attempts to use the subject matter of his books as evidence against him. His literary earnings were paralyzed by the IRS; there were liens on his houses.

The book that resulted from this struggle moves from detailed autobiography to a discussion of our national destiny. In its resentment of just about everything in America, it bears a certain resemblance to Richard Nixon's 1952 Checkers speech. However, while Nixon defended himself against charges of misuse of funds by lachrymose pleading, innuendo, and dramatizing of his own position, Wilson depends throughout on an analysis of the meaning of government's power.

The story begins with one man's unhappiness and resentment. The power unit that Wilson indicts forced him to provide a detailed account of his expenses: he was told by an IRS agent that he was spending too much money on liquor and that he could not afford to buy a bed for his dog. Wilson's marriages threw doubt on his financial dealings: "It is apparently un-American to be married four times." Wilson uses the material of his case not for a personal drama but as a way into the question of "What Rip Van Winkle Woke Up To"—the plight of the working professional with no depletion allowances and no "large scale juggling devices." As he develops his theme, he describes his position as the writer at the mercy of "Bureaucratic Theology." The "theologians" of the IRS have devised distinctions of scholastic subtlety to control the lives, values, and interests of the citizenry. "Deductions," in Wilson's view, are the government's way of shaping lives.

What right has the government to say what expenses are and are not "legitimate"? This is the realm of "psychic value," with which no government can really deal. It is an insufferable impertinence of the federal government to ask why I have entertained my guests or why I have chosen to travel—to say nothing of how many times I have been married, whom I have voted for, and whether or not I buy my dog a bed.

Despite the cane-brandishing stance of the old fogy, Wilson does not become enmeshed in his own situation. *The Cold War and the Income Tax* soon proceeds to problems larger than one man's miseries.

The first of these is the monolithic character of government itself. In one of his best chapters, "The Point of View of a Former Socialist," he explains his own attitude toward the modern state. Here the reader is listening to an analyst who reflects on the course of his own development and does so without self-congratulation or peevishness. After admitting that he was "naive enough at thirty-one to take seriously Lenin's prediction" that government bureaucracy would give way to more democratic organization and that the state would "wither away" and "cease to harass the individual," he proceeds to show how such thinking completely missed the tendencies in both the Soviet Union and the United States. The power drive in both countries was fully developed even in the thirties—in America, of course, it was the growth of government agencies that interfered on behalf of the unprotected; in the Soviet Union it was the Stalinist bureaucracy devised to protect the state from counterrevolutionaries. But in both countries Wilson sees the crushing force of supernationalism, the force that Americans felt most strongly from the Civil War onward and that Russians felt during and after the revolution. The "former" socialist connects the country of hope—the Soviet Union and its heroic founding fathers—with the worst features in his own country. Questionable as such a connection may be, and much as it may suggest that he shoots from the hip in his criticism of modern American governmental power, the book does not fall into the error of celebrating the glories of socialism or the purity of his own position: Wilson treats all power units with contempt and he portrays himself with gruff candor. No socialist saint or ideologue, he appears as a man who finds America an uncomfortable place, who is determined to earn as little as he can in order to deprive the government of its taxes, and who fully intends to stay put and complain.

Wilson shows himself in a distinctly unheroic light, speaking vehemently, but always afraid of Uncle Sam. His contribution to the struggle against government power is more a matter of personal candor than of organized resistance. Those who did refuse "to lie down"—Wilson's favorite way of describing heroism—let themselves in for horrifying consequences. "The Case of Major Eatherly" is one of the most moving chapters in the book. Eatherly, the pilot who commanded the bombing of Hiroshima and Nagasaki, is the quintessential battler in Wilson's story. This military man went public with his guilt feelings, his anger, and his sense of horror, and he wound up institutionalized. Wilson meticulously picks through this case and presents us with material that supports his generalizations about the brutality of the power drive: Eatherly is silenced and sequestered in a manner that is chillingly suggestive of the fate of Soviet dissidents.

The most original aspect of Wilson's polemic against Uncle Sam is his cold-eyed attitude toward the victims of government. Wilson does not set up a righteous argument in which he presents American citizens as blameless. Indeed, he sees the people who are taxed and bamboozled as part of the problem: after seeing what happens to Eatherly and other heroic men, they sink into moral irresponsibility and intellectual torpor. The world of Hecate County with its evasions and illusions, its escape through drink and sex, is updated in this latest book of bad news. Our laxity and fear, which Wilson freely acknowledges as part of his own reaction, give us little to look forward to: "We may hope for a moment of enjoyment from bottled and pre-mixed cocktails or an outdoor grill in the suburbs or a movie that shows lovers in bed or someone getting lashed or bashed." Our stupefied state will in turn feed the disease of power lust: as Eatherly and other protesters go down in defeat, our capacity for resistance is weakened; as we are weakened and demoralized, government is emboldened. The grim news of *The Cold War and the Income Tax* is that this weakening of fiber seems to increase with each year. Wilson's polemic—intemperate and often irascible—is nevertheless worthy to be considered an important document in the history of liberal warning. Like J. S. Mill in *On Liberty,* Wilson expresses fears about a nation-state that can dwarf its citizens and render them passive.

The pressure of the state is also the theme of Wilson's books about the American Indians. In his presentation of peoples who have denied the authority of the state and attempted to live as independent aliens in our midst, Wilson sees some hope. The radical disengagement of the Iroquois and the Zuni from their American neighbors, for example, is inspiriting at a time when Wilson perceives a general flabbiness in the lives of Americans. *Apologies to the Iroquois* and "Zuni," an extended essay in *Red, Black, Blond and Olive,* are both about tribes that refused to "lie down"—the Iroquois maintained that they were not American citizens and refused to get off their land at Schoharie Creek; the Zuni existed quite apart from the Sun Belt prosperity of New Mexico and prided themselves on a heritage of missionary killing. Wilson presents both tribes as arresting examples of dignity in the midst of materialism and moral compromise.

Apologies to the Iroquois takes as its overriding thematic purpose the contrasts between the acquisitive mentality of the American and the spiritual-aristocratic ideals of the Indian. The Iroquois have been treated as children by the United States government because they are unable to grasp the advantages of owning private property and holding legal title. In fact, the Iroquois reject our whole system of property arrangements, along with our ideas about trade and profit; the cash nexus has little significance for a tribe that has a gentleman-warrior standard of excellence. The Iroquois, Wilson emphasizes, are generous, uncalculating, and contemptuous of middle-class prosperity. Their shabby material surroundings are totally at variance with the conspicuous consumption of modern Americans and express their absorption in spiritual matters.

The book in many ways is Wilson's most optimistic report of the post–World War II period on the persistence of humane rebellion. Wilson writes about Iroquois men breaking into a museum to "feed" Indian masks that had been alienated from the tribe by the greedy, art-collecting white man. He attends the Little Water Ceremony and feels great respect for a kind of piety that antedates Christianity. He researches the work of a great Indian religious thinker who sought to establish a moral code to protect his people from the white man's liquor and his corrupt values. Throughout the book he searches out symbols of resistance—whether scalp locks protesting the "mechanical uniformity imposed by industrial civilization" or independent Indian council meetings held in opposition to New York State's idea of having Indian puppet governments.

The Indian leaders take their places in the Wilson gallery of resisters of tyranny. Mad Bear, a Tuscarora leader, wins Wilson's respect by assuming the role of a latter-day democratic revolutionary: this leader's dramatic and decisive manner recalls the power and imagination of Trotsky. On one occasion, he "led four hundred Indians into court and tore up the summons that had been served to them" for not paying state income tax. This man, with his "self-controlled audacity," his tactical successes, and his "aspect of pugnacious durability" is a more encouraging example of nay-saying than anyone in the defeated white world of *The Cold War and the Income Tax*. Wilson sees the Tuscarora themselves as champions in the struggle against the demon of centralization: the dramatic high point of the book presents the way they won a judgment in court against the most imperious figure in the state, Robert Moses, builder of parks and symbol of grand-scale annexation.

Despite the excitement and hope of *Apologies to the Iroquois*, it is less rich and strange than the Zuni essays and more of a straight job of reporting than Wilson's finest reflective essays. While the Zuni pieces are charged with anger at the American empire, they are also filled with the ambivalence and tension, color and mystery of complex works like *To the Finland Station* and *Axel's Castle*. Wild men rather than New York State neighbors, these Zuni inspire Wilson to compare their rites to the fierce vitality of Stravinsky and Diaghilev: describing the resistance of modern art to conventional ways of feeling and thinking is one way Wilson has of conveying Zuni life. Their village is likened to a foreign country, "newer and older" than Europe itself since these people live without cultural reference to our civilization. Wilson's reaction to the elaborate ceremony of Shálako, the coming of gods into houses—the centerpiece of Zuni religious life—is one of awe. The blazing light and dancing seem to summon "elemental power" for the people: "It seems as if the dancer, by his pounding, were really generating energy for the Zunis; by his discipline, strengthening their fortitude; by his endurance, guaranteeing their permanence." Wilson can "withstand its [the dance's] effect" only "with effort." This is an especially odd statement from a reporter who has withstood and criticized everything from symbolist obscurity to communist piety and Calvinist fanaticism. But no sooner does he describe his attraction than he pulls back and retreats into his most characteristic qualifying skepticism: "One did not want to rejoin the Zuni in their primitive nature cult; and it was hardly worthwhile for a Protestant to have stripped off the mummeries of Rome in order to fall a victim to an agile young man in a ten foot mask." While he disengages himself from the mythic and ritualistic part of Zuni life, he cannot forget the consequences that flow into these people's communal life from belief. Fortitude, staunch resistance to progress, and the pursuit of nonmaterial happiness stand out luminously against the landscape of compromise.

During his lengthy campaign against American progress and centralization, Wilson directed his own little blue light of anger and disdain at writers whose talents have been brought under the dominion of larger institutions. His treatment of Henry Luce's *Time* in his 1944 essay "Thoughts on Being Bibliographed" is an intemperate but significant attack on what he considers slick style and cynical attitude. The essay deals with the problem that he would develop at length in *Patriotic Gore:* the reduction of problems and personalities that takes place when highly skillful and efficient writers neglect human emotion and complexity. The relationship between Timese and "the language of responsibility"— with its correctitude and its lack of idiosyncrasy and individuality—is clear: "the men who put the various points of view of *Time* together appear to have been mashed down and to figure in what they print only as blurred streaks of coloration that blot the machine finished surface." *Time* portrays people "as manikins, sometimes cocky, sometimes busy, sometimes zealous, sometimes silly, sometimes gruesome, but in most cases quite infrahuman." Indeed this dead style calls Bierce's prose to mind. While the characterizing here is dated in terms of the magazine we now read, the forceful diagnosis of a problem in modern writing is of great use to any critic faced with the task of judging the sleek surfaces of popular magazines that make people into spectacles and world events into all-too-intelligible entertainments.

These slaps at the corporate style of reporting are only part of the total campaign against the processing of prose. Some 25 years later he was denouncing another aspect of centralization, the Modern Language Association, a scholarly organization that was in the process of annexing classic American works for its specialized editions. The writer who spent the fifties and sixties explaining the machinations of government and pressure groups now undertook an analysis of the politics of literary scholarship in *The Fruits of the MLA*. The impolite tone of the book, with its excoriating irony directed at pedantic professors, is the same tone we have already heard in *The Cold War and the Income Tax*.

The occasion for this outburst against the world of the mind was the publication of aforementioned editions of American writers. In the income tax book Wilson had himself advocated that government subsidize good, cheap editions of classics; he had in mind that the average reader would be able to learn from them about the heritage of nineteenth-century literature. Wilson's idea, which he drew up carefully with the help of the young publisher Jason Epstein, died on the vine. Some years later, however, the MLA started producing editions of the American classics that completely abandoned the spirit of the Wilson proposal and at the same time tried to impress the scholarly world with service rendered to our national letters. Bulky, overly detailed, footnote-infested editions of works of dubious value began to appear. Their price tags shut out the average reader just as their apparatus did.

In his essay, Wilson enters the arena filled with personal resentment and energized by his own literary code. This battle of the books is first of all fought by a man who sensed a conspiracy. The MLA, a powerful pressure group, "had a strong and determined lobby to further its own designs"; the "representatives of the MLA had attempted to discourage our project and had, it seems, very soon succeeded." Even more important than the grudge is the MLA's offense against writing and reading: the trinity of force, ease, and lucidity that informed Wilson's style did not preside over the world of professional scholars. The readers of one of these editions might be greeted "with thirty-five pages of textual commentary which record the variations of nine of the existing texts." They might be asked to interest themselves in variations in spelling and hyphenation or small discrepancies between a writer's diary and a page of fiction. They might also be asked to read a book like William Dean Howells's *Their Wedding Journey*. But more serious than these charges is the implicit argument of Wilson's book, that the scholarly industry has forgotten what literature is. Pleasure is completely bypassed by the editors—and Wilson attacks them as he has attacked other obscurantists.

The religious fervor of "hyphen-hunting" is the latest echo of the IRS "theologians" and the inspired men and women of the Civil War period. The average reader interested in the style and sensibility of a writer is considered unfit to judge the mysteries of scholarship just as the average taxpayer and the rational survivalist are considered unfit to judge the mysteries of tax codes and defense allocations. To question the great centralized production of America's classics is to be guilty of "ignorance, unreason, infantilism and meanness." Wilson glories in such charges, indeed wears them like badges of honor. They indicate that rational inquiry and criticism of his kind meet with haughty dismissals from those who have institutionalized power.

From the postwar period until the late sixties, Wilson's evaluation of the American scene is essentially a brilliant demolition job; he carries on a stripping and shredding operation as he analyzes the power drive. Like a latter-day Jeremy Bentham, he demolishes the rationales of institutions and group mentalities, exposes the underpinnings and confusions of national life. But it is a further measure of Wilson's complexity as an artist and reporter that he carried out this grim, essentially negative job in the same period that he was building a life-availing, counterbalancing world of meaning in other books.

Chapter Seven
What the Scrolls Said

During the years when Wilson was shrinking myths and attacking pieties, he was also building an ethic of his own, a moral pension fund for his old age. At a time when he was documenting the power drive, he took several opportunities to express his private code of living, a series of loosely formulated precepts about endurance, order and continuity, living well, and the value of human contact. The first major opportunity to be what Paul has called "a spokesman-at-large for the human spirit"[1] came in 1954 when Wilson went to Israel to study the Dead Sea Scrolls. These documents became the occasion for studying the idea of Jewishness and the way it impinged on his own Gentile world. In 1956, he gave the public *A Piece of My Mind*, a collection of essays that commemorated his 60th year and left his personal imprint on a gathering of moral issues. *Upstate* appeared in 1971 and completed Wilson's view of moral life by using the history of the old stone house at Talcottville as a means for exploring his feelings about himself and the world.

Wilson's construction of a durable self, of course, is not a matter of these later books alone. *To the Finland Station*, while giving us a 200-year narrative sweep, dwells reverently on the characters of Marx and Lenin, their capacity for resistance, and their refusal to compromise; their homes are holy places and their works have an ethical significance for Wilson that the horrors of Stalinism could not erase. But in the postwar period Wilson saw these revolutionary ideals as quite distant from the realities of the Soviet state and the American empire. In addition, there were other losses: the great modern writers were no longer on the scene; friends like Fitzgerald were gone, while others like Edna Millay were wasting away.

Wilson not only assaulted the worst aspects of the times, he also toughened up by stating where he stood on personal morality. This part of his postwar writing is foreshadowed by a small essay, "A Dissenting Opinion on Kafka" (1946), a combative discussion of consequences and values in literature rather than a piece of analytic criticism. Although Wilson was by no means unique in attacking Kafka's reputation as a moralist, he did so in an especially candid way: "Franz Kafka has been looming on the literary world like the meteorological phenomenon called the Brocken spectre: a human shadow thrown on the mist in such a way that it seems monstrous and remote when it may really be quite close at hand, and with a rainbow halo around it." Kafka, Wilson argues, has been conceived of by American intellectuals as a writer of spiritual fables, a sage and poet who belongs in the company of Joyce and Proust. Wilson opens fire on this idea and by so doing establishes his own position. Wilson believes that Kafka's spiritual stature has been overestimated: the "spiritual charge" was "insulated" and "eventually nullified" by the way Kafka lived and thought. While we might at first think of Kafka as fitting the wound and bow idea—and thus being an important figure for a critic concerned with trauma—we are soon led to see that Wilson regards the spirit of the Prague novelist as quite different from that of a writer like Dickens. One of Kafka's most famous aphorisms, expressing his peculiar and tragic sense of twentieth-century life, is a distillation of all that Wilson does not stand for: "One must not cheat anybody, not even the world of its triumph." Wilson feels that the author of such a statement is lacking in "vitality," "faith," and "the will to get his own back." He argues that "the denationalized, discouraged, disaffected, disabled Kafka, though for a moment he may frighten or amuse us, can in the end only let us down."

Is this a philistine attitude directed against a sensitive, complex artist who is struggling tragically in a hostile environment? Has Wilson lost touch with his own sympathies for injured artists? There can be no denying that this essay contains a certain amount of muscle flexing: "But what are writers here for if it is not to cheat the world of its triumph?" is hardly a subtle formulation. Yet the question does not suggest that artists should conceal anxieties or scale down their visions; it also implies a disdain for conformity and conventional response in aesthetics and politics that is wholly at odds with the philistine notion that the artist should confirm popular beliefs.

Whether we accept or reject Wilson's verdict on Kafka,[2] we cannot fail to see the evidence that led to his conclusions. Kafka is involved with "assimilating men to beasts," and frequently his characters, burdened as they are with guilt and anxiety, "can neither dare nor know." Baffled by the conditions of modern life and laboring under strange personal burdens, they go down in defeat. Wilson—whether because he is afraid of Kafka's negative vision or repelled by it—will not allow that the creator of such characters can be thought of as a great religious-spiritual writer. Kafka—the writer whom William Barrett calls "the saint of spiritual anemia"[3]—once said that he represented the "negative elements" of his age. Such an outlook was in itself an assault on Wilson's most preciously held beliefs: order, progress, the efficacy of thought and work, the idea of completion and accomplishment. As a modern writer Kafka could not stand in the Wilson pantheon because, unlike Joyce and Proust, he resisted the heroic role of the artist as bringer of coherence. In an entry in Wilson's notebooks *The Forties*, we learn that Kafka was a candidate for inclusion in *The Wound and the Bow*. The name "Kafka" is followed by a question mark; he never found a place in the book about trauma and resistance. Wilson's vigorous dismissal of a great writer is certainly not one of his more sensitive moments as a critic, but at the same time it is an honest admission of standards, and, given Wilson's fears about the castle of self-absorption, it should not seem disconsonant with his earlier literary essays. In the 1946 essay Wilson gives way to an irritability that was present in his judgments from the start of his career.

The central ideas of the Kafka essay echo throughout Wilson's works of moral criticism; each work, however, has its own tones, its own value, and its own special texture. The first major sustained books about resisting defeat are contained in *Israel and the Dead Sea Scrolls*, a volume of 1954 sketches about Jewish culture as well as Wilson's famous analysis of the ancient Scrolls. Leon Edel says of the work on the Scrolls that "no book quite like this has been written in our century."[4] It links "a popular narrative to high erudition" in such a way as to make readers vitally concerned with customs and scholarly problems that at first seem obscure and remote from everyday life. Partly "a modern Sherlock Holmes story," but principally a writer's story of belief, the book is about Wilson's discovery of the Jewish contribution to Western thought.

In a modest spirit of inquiry, Wilson describes how he began to study Hebrew in 1952 at the Princeton Theological Seminary. Spurred on by curiosity about an ancient language rather than by some plan for a new book, he expressed the exhilaration of discovering the "intellectual and spiritual mystery" of the Hebrew characters. He emerged from his studies saying "I am no Semitic scholar."[5] When he came to write about the Scrolls, he consistently emphasized his areas of incompetence: his lack of acquaintance with the range of biblical scholarship, his alien's perspective, and his problems with basic reading. Yet he plunged into Judaic studies not to resolve any scholarly questions or provide any masterly interpretations of difficult issues, but to explain his personal responses.

The chapters in *Israel*, besides containing reports on different features of ancient and modern life, are a reflection on the themes of endurance and strength. As Wilson describes his own experiences in "On First Reading Genesis," we are led into a fascinating world of symbols, one in which "the whole language is intensely purposeful, full of determination to survive by force or by wit." Wilson, like Keats in "On First Looking into Chapman's Homer," surveys the realms of a text and looks with his own "wild surmise" at the prospect of a new intellectual world, one in which the verb tenses themselves express an idea of eternity. Without our conception of the present moment, the Hebrew language is the perfect object for the attentions of a writer at odds with his time and country. In learning to write Hebrew characters during his studies, he relates "a feeling of vicarious authority as one traces the portentous syllables." The characters "march on through our modern events as if they were invulnerable, eternal."

The stories, as well as the language, cause Wilson to meditate on the theme of endurance. In the case of his analysis of Jacob, the patriarch who struggled with God, Wilson presents a Hebrew scene in terms that reflect back on the Promethean values in *To the Finland Station*. Jacob, who was maimed by God in a contest, is thereafter to be called Israel— striver with God. From this story Wilson concludes that the name the Jews gave their nation contains "the idea that they had conquered, at a maiming cost, some share in the power of God." The "share" is not clearly described, but at different times Wilson refers to the "aspect of eternity" under which the Jew lives and the awareness of "the conscience that begins to dignify him, that seems to tower above him." The eternity idea of course puts the Jews at odds with the quotidian world, and in itself is a social disability that confers a kind of strength and identity. Wilson looks with awe at the "Guardians of the City," an ultra-Orthodox sect whose members refuse to acknowledge the state of Israel because they must await the Messiah. The idea of conscience is described in a vivid way as Wilson analyzes the differences between the easily visualized holy places of ancient Greece and Rome and the holy places of the Jews, which are "hard to imagine." Wilson the literary man is excited by the fact that words, not images, are the way the Jews have of preserving and handing down their idea of conscience.

One of *Israel*'s best chapters, "The Fiction of S. Y. Agnon," shows Wilson the synthetic thinker combining the tasks of moral and literary criticism; his reasons for disapproving of Kafka's world view are amplified as he analyzes another Jewish writer who employs fantasy. Agnon's writing—a combination of intense spirituality and homely detail about village life in Poland—is inspiriting for Wilson because, unlike Kafka, Agnon has an abiding faith and love. His characters live in simple settings but imagine "in terms of a universe that has no real locale or date except possibly in the hoped-for return to that distant idealized Israel toward which the most pious among them have never ceased to yearn." Along with Wilson's Wandering Jew in *The Little Blue Light*, these fictional people are sustained by the knowledge that they are on an intelligible spiritual journey. Kafka's journeys are, of course, always tragic wanderings in an unintelligible world. In Wilson's preferences we see not only a kind of moral assertion and turning away from the ambiguity of literary modernism but also a growing coolness toward the problematic nature of twentieth-century storytelling. The author who once celebrated symbolism has now moved into a phase in which he puts his trust in more straightforward, old-fashioned allegory.[6]

Another aspect of Wilson's later thought comes through as he remarks that "Agnon never blights his characters, and he cannot resist a miracle." That Wilson has apparently strayed from the path of skepticism here should not be taken as a sign that he is at all possessed by an idea of heavenly salvation. What he has found is a love and human warmth as well as a belief in endurance that cannot be demystified without shrinking the stature of man himself. The Agnon essay shows Wilson closing the gap between his intellectual needs and standards and his need for human contact.

After hearing such values asserted, the reader is better able to understand the nature of the more complex work, *The Dead Sea Scrolls*. The book is essentially about endurance and dedication: it fuses these themes into a narrative that at first seems like a scholarly exploration.

Wilson tells the story of how the Scrolls—which include scriptures and the Manual of Discipline of the Essene sect—were discovered, came into the possession of a Syrian archbishop, and generated controversy among Jews and Christians. This Syrian archbishop, known as the Metropolitan Samuel, persisted in his efforts to gain recognition for the antiquity and authenticity of the documents. At first scholars from several camps said that the works could not date from the first century A. D. Wilson's story becomes one in which some Jewish scholars resisted the Scrolls because of the ways they might damage the authority of the Old Testament text, and some Christian scholars resisted them because the Essenes, a pre-Christian ascetic monastic community led by a radical Jewish Teacher of Righteousness, seemed to pose a threat to the uniqueness of Christ's teachings. The Metropolitan becomes a symbol of integrity and endurance in the book as he takes the Scrolls from scholar to scholar, hoping for understanding of a unique find. Later on, other intrepid and extraordinary figures gave their attention to the Essene issue. Père Roland de Vaux reconstructed the daily life of the monks; André Dupont-Sommer, a Sorbonne Hebrew scholar, brought his secular perspective to bear on studying the Teacher of Righteousness and inspired Wilson with his devotion to historical scholarship rather than to theology. David Flusser, a volatile polymath living in Israel, captivated Wilson by telling him that the idea of being one of the Elect—a key doctrine of the Essene sect—is the foundation for the teaching of Paul, Calvin, and Marx. Finally, Wilson celebrates the determination of the Israeli general Yadin, the man responsible for getting the Scrolls into the Jerusalem museum. Daring to know and daring to persist with one's knowledge—these are the recurrent themes in the lives of the scholars Wilson met.

Wilson's overarching concern in handling the subtle issues of scholarship is his interest in continuity as a kind of morality. Just as he retold Genesis in *Israel* to emphasize the Jewish idea of ongoing dedication, he explores the radical Essene sect to find out how its doctrines and way of life make Christianity historically comprehensible. As a follower of rivers in "The Old Stone House" and a searcher after origins in *Axel's Castle* and *To the Finland Station*, he now looks for the sources of Messianic teaching in history. In making connections between the Essenes and Jesus, he is not, however, engaged in cheap demolition work. He leaves it to the orthodox believers to decide on the importance of Christ's words; he insists only that Christ took his place in human history—an idea that no enlightened Christian finds offensive. In describing the Essene sect, he writes of their brotherhood, sacrifice, resistance to the Jewish community, and celibacy: this is the historical matrix out of which some of Jesus' teachings came. "It would appear, in other words, that Jesus may well have found for himself, by the teaching of the Dead Sea sect, a special Messianic role, the pattern of a martyr's career which he accepted, to which he aspired." For Wilson, the Essene monastery, "More than Bethlehem or Nazareth, [is] the cradle of Christianity." But such a connection should not be taken to mean that Wilson is equating Essenism with Jesus' teachings. In a finely discriminating passage—one that is as sensitive to distinctions as his writings about Marx and other socialists—he shows how a historical relationship is not identity:

Anyone who goes to the Gospels from . . . the literature of the Dead Sea
sect must feel at once the peculiar genius of Jesus and be struck by the
impossibility of falling in with the worst tendencies of insensitive modern
scholarship and accounting for everything in the Gospels in terms of
analogies and precedents.

At odds with vulgar reductionists in approaching Jesus' teachings,
he is nevertheless opposed to the Christian ethos as well as to the Jews'
devotion to their God. While "aware that, for those of real religious
vocation, their religious transcendences and revelations are as real as
anything else in their lives," Wilson has felt "no moment of exaltation"
that brings him "close to God."[7] Although he can turn to poets' illumi-
nations and be "moved and impressed" by Dante's vision, he has contempt for religious exaltation when it is joined to the careers of charis-
matic leaders. His book on the Scrolls ends in doubt: after all that he
has taken from the Judaic tradition—ideas of endurance, resistance,
moral authority, and faith in words—be rejects the prophetic mentality
outright. He concludes his treatment of God-filled men by attacking
Joseph Smith, the founder of Mormonism. This rather questionable figure, given his reputation as a fanatic and teller of tall tales, is Wilson's
example of the spiritual, righteous mentality. Hardly a fair representative of the spiritual life, Smith is nevertheless the man Wilson chooses
to bring to our attention as we reach the end of his book on the Judaic
idea of righteousness. The growth of religious belief in the West starts
with the Jews and continues into the Christian sects as an "obsessive
ideal projected by the human imagination." After explaining his values
in the terms of ancient and modern Jewish endurance, he disengages
himself from the mystical and doctrinal aspects of both Judaism and
Christianity. While Jews and Christians cherish ideas of salvation, Wilson chooses to retain only the ideal of resilient character and reverence
for language.

A Piece of My Mind (1956) reemphasizes the moral values of continuity and resistance as it carries over some of the topics of *The Dead Sea
Scrolls*. This time the tone is more personal as Wilson relates his perceptions of Jewish studies, the Bible, and the Jewish impact on American
thought.[8] As a writer whose grandfather was a Presbyterian minister,
Wilson was heir to a tradition that had many affinities with Judaism.
Bible study and the pride of being set apart from less serious people
were very definite features of his early life. On the one hand, his attitude

toward a grandmother who exerted moral pressure on him each Sunday is very clearly negative; he explains how at Princeton he revolted against the Hebraizing of such Puritan relatives and felt drawn instead to the classical, with its values of beauty and intellectual inquiry. Such an attraction, on the other hand, did not kill what he later refers to as the Protestant's "atavistic obsession" with Hebrew literature and Jewish culture. In a section that is a fascinating exploration of the Puritan mind, Wilson writes about New Englanders and their use of the moral vocabulary of the Old Testament. This obsession with covenants, with the New World as Canaan, and even with George III as pharaoh has a profound effect on Wilson. He was drawn to his forebears' Hebraic frames of reference while he began to worry about the way that extreme fascination with Judaism—particularly with the idea of a strong and alien people—can turn to fear and anti-Semitism. Wilson the shrinker of myths takes on a gallery of obsessed American thinkers, employing once again the irony of *Patriotic Gore*. Otherwise intelligent men fell prey to a weird belief in Jewish omnipresence and omnipotence. It is almost as if in *A Piece of My Mind* Wilson is ridding himself of one of the ancestral demons that haunted him. He opens the closet of genteel American letters and exposes writers' fantasies to the light of day. He shows us James Russell Lowell finding Jews "hiding" behind Gentile-sounding names, or his hero John Jay Chapman swinging from extravagant praise of Jewish cultural achievement to snide anti-Semitism, or Wendell Barrett arguing that, since the New Englander came from counties in England that once had a good many Jews, New England Puritans were really of Jewish blood!

After airing such nonsense, he stands back from his subject and evaluates his own feeling about Jewish culture and belief. His principal attachment to Judaism is no matter of romantic attraction, no idealization. Instead it is a kind of relief from Christian mythology. The absence of Christ and of saints and images is bracing to a writer in flight from the display, the insistence, and the public power of large institutions. Judaism constitutes an emptiness that leaves room for reflection.

A Piece of My Mind unfortunately overplays its attack on Christian culture. It becomes not merely a candid declaration of feelings, but a vulgar, philistine attack—laced with humor of the coarsest sort—on the splendors of Christendom. Writing with the bumptious attitude of a character out of Dickens, he claims to "have derived a good deal more benefit of the civilizing as well as of the inspirational kind from the admirable American bathroom" than from the cathedrals of Europe:

The cathedrals, with their distant domes, their long aisles and their high groinings, do add stature to human strivings; their chapels do give privacy for prayer. But the bathroom, too, shelters the spirit, it tranquilizes and reassures, in surroundings of celestial whiteness, where the pipes and faucets gleam and the mirror makes another liquid surface, which will render you, shaved, rubbed and brushed, a nobler and more winning appearance. Here, too, you may sing, recite, refresh yourself with brief readings, just as you do in church; and the fact that you do it without a priest and not as a member of a congregation is, from my point of view, an advantage. It encourages self-dependence and prepares one to face the world fortified, firm on one's feet, serene and with a mind like a diamond.

The writer who mounted his criticism of Kafka, of Marxists, and of Christian scholars who were blind to historical scholarship has here lost his balance as he horses around with serious ideas. It is also dismaying to observe the scourge of American commercialism lapsing into complacency.

His chapter called "Sex" is even more disturbing. It has a creepy, almost fanatical tone that contrasts markedly with the irony and honest sexuality in *Memoirs of Hecate County*. He directs a polemic at "educated people" and their attitudes: "The sentimentalities, romanticisms, idealisms that make up so much of modern literature have concealed from such people the pattern and the purpose of the mating of human beings, which is basically identical with those of the mating of the other animals." From this proposition he goes on to treat the "appalling degree" to which modern writers have emphasized people who "are incapable of experiencing the full cycle of courtship, fruition, relief." The "literature of sterility"—including the "renunciations of Henry James, the hysterical orgasms of Lawrence, the impotent and obsessive suspicions of Proust"—represents "the dislocations of the reproductive instinct." Wilson advances the notion that such weaklings ultimately destroy themselves and their alternative ways of life. He awaits a new age of eugenics. He insists that a "new elite can be produced from supervised breeding" and that we can be "saved from the dominance of mediocrity and from the letting down of all standards."

Wilson asks us not to regard his opinions as a reemergence of the attitudes of the German Youth Movement but rather as a search for excellence. He wants to remind us that the pretensions of aristocracies "were never perhaps completely false; but that door seems closed forever." And yet the intellectual difficulties and futilities, not to mention the dangers, of his opinions seem to sprout up everywhere. First, he aligns himself with a tradition of social breeding that extends from Malthus to Herbert Spencer and Hitler: his worries about the mediocrity of the species belong with those of the woolliest and most frightening thinkers of the past two centuries.[9] The idea of an aristocracy has also been a last refuge for thinkers and writers who have exhausted their talents or despaired about the possibilities for social improvement. Some, like Thomas Carlyle, have wound up ranting at the democratic process and the evils of an Iron Age; others like Ezra Pound have spewed hate in works of art and taken their place in the history of fanaticism. While Wilson is more guarded than either Carlyle or Pound, he is nevertheless reckless—and strangely untrue to his own best observations. Eugenics would constitute an obstruction to our appreciation of the whole accidental, anomalous, and unmeasured world of art and artists. In advancing eugenic theories, Wilson is effectively turning against some of his own most sensitive readings of wounds and achievements. Dickens and Proust—two writers whose afflictions are so much a part of their art—would become cases rather than the heroic exemplars that Wilson once presented to us. As for the relationship of eugenics to Wilson's view of the state, it is clear that he has not reflected on the agency most likely to help us toward the brave new world: "that son of a bitch Uncle Sam" would, in the world of the future, be doing more than collecting taxes and waging war.

When Wilson leaves the realms of "a better world" behind and returns to his own observations about experience, he is a much more convincing writer and moralist. "The Author at Sixty" shows old fogyism closing in as Wilson begins to sort out what he likes and dislikes about modern life. Although he claims to feed on memories, he seems as aware and involved with life as he did in the days when he crossed the country looking for stories. Wearing the mask of the fogy—unable to abide radio or television or involve himself with contemporary books or conflicts—he discusses two aspects of moral life, continuity and standards.

Being connected with the past for Wilson means looking for role models or great men. Wilson announces his moral touchstone at the beginning of the essay: "as an American, I am more or less in the eighteenth century." The idea of republican virtue—public-spiritedness and resistance to commercial opportunism—begins with the Founding Fathers and threads its way through the lives of the more important presidents. In an earlier chapter on the United States, Wilson has already explained the republican ethos: it is the attitude and thinking of men who "have a stake in the success of our system," who "share the responsibility to carry on its institutions," and who give the system dignity and "make it work." Its exemplars are men like Jefferson, Lincoln, and Franklin Roosevelt. Wilson's point in his meditations is that he has sought a way of establishing contact with this part of the American political tradition at a time when lesser men and their constricted views have come to prevail. The man whose view of life comes from a background in party politics (Harry Truman) or the expert in some field who has little understanding of politics or economics (Dwight Eisenhower) is a threatening presence in American life. Furthermore, Wilson sees "dislocations" and "disruptions," a breaking of faith with the eighteenth-century tradition of civic virtue and public service. A Truman is first and foremost a loyal party man. The party "has been for him not only his profession, but also his college, his church and his club; it has even become somehow his country." Such a man "inhabits so different a world from the man of high civic conscience that the outlook and the language of the latter are hardly intelligible to him." The Eisenhower type is inert and therefore cannot be expected to do more than favor conservative elements. What all this means to Wilson is that the connection with ideals of probity and progress are becoming increasingly difficult to trace in the American landscape.

In "The Author at Sixty" he reflects on how his old stone house is a symbol of the continuous tradition. Whether, as some critics have maintained, this turning to the personal life is a turning away from America, a retreat into the self, or whether it is the healthy response of a public-spirited man is open to much debate.[10] Seen from a different angle, however, Wilson's stance is part of his career as a moralist. Gratified by "the sense of my continuity"—his place in Talcottville among old books and the remnants of the eighteenth century—and "fortified by this place and its people to withstand many fakes and distractions," he has found his own equivalent of the strength of Jewish tradition. As a writer who spent his life working on topics of public concern, in Talcottville he becomes a private man and moralist in a distinctly impersonal and public way: he is never involved with personality, but rather with getting in touch with currents of thought and a common life larger than himself.

The question of standards—refusing to capitulate in a world of party men and passive leaders—involves Wilson in the story of his father's life. The troubled, wounded, melancholy parent provides not the usual occasion for rebellion, but a model of dignity and resistance. The Gilded Age of the elder Wilson's young manhood was a period in which many professional men either put their services at the disposal of big business or wasted their spirit in fruitless resistance or self-indulgence. Wilson proposes his father's way of life as a painful but honorable alternative to selling out or going crazy or sinking into sensuality. At bottom, the elder Wilson's code was the Puritan's obsession with being one of the elect; in ordinary terms—the ones that Wilson uses—it is an intense fear of not "amounting" to something. Wilson elsewhere recalls how his father would watch his school progress and sometimes accuse him of "weltering in a Dead Sea of mediocrity." The father presented the example of distinction by pursuing goals that were disconsonant with big business success: he insisted, as his son later would, on amounting to something in his own way and on his own terms. "The Author at Sixty" describes the father's pursuits and positions: service to the community, old-fashioned devotion to a profession, belief in human progress through work rather than through financial or political schemes, curiosity about other cultures, disdain for suburban pleasures and good living, belief in minority causes. The reader of Wilson's previous works sees this sketch of the father as a program and a way of life for the son. Amounting to something in his father's way was Wilson's highest moral ideal. When Wilson says that his father "got through with honor that period from 1880–1920!" he also means that he himself made it through the age of Hecate County and the postwar years. The father's moral capital was intact and available for the son.

"The Author at Sixty" provides a transition to the book Wilson worked on in the late 1960s. *Upstate* (1971) is sprung out of the implications of his 1956 conclusion: "Am I, then, in a pocket of the past? I do not necessarily believe it. I may find myself here at the center of things—since the center can only be in one's head—and my feelings and thoughts may be shared by many." The statement is packed with the conflicts of a lifetime: the castle of one's mind versus the concerns of humanity, the worries about establishing contact with others expressed in "necessarily" and "may," the center versus the pocket of the past. The paradox of the statement is that his thoughts and experiences, derived from recollection in solitude, may be "shared," that being at a distance from activity may be a way of sharing.

Upstate is about a writer who has found a way of living this paradox: it is at once Wilson's most aloof and most engaged work. In the simplest sense it is concerned with how he removed himself from the flow of literary life and family routine for about 20 summers, about how he left commitments and complications behind in favor of life in an abandoned house in a remote village. The house turns out to be not only a vantage point from which to observe America but also a location in which to experience a new kind of sharing, a trading of thoughts and feelings with ancestors and neighbors. "I like the feeling that I am occupying the largest and most distinguished house in the town—though the population of Talcottville is now hardly more than eighty people, that everybody knows me and takes me for granted—that I can say or do whatever I please, with the town at my door and all about me."

In its tones and its approach to American life, *Upstate* is a book that explores social customs, literature, and its author's mind without Wilson's characteristic interrogation and arrowlike precision. Unlike *Apologies to the Iroquois* or *The American Earthquake* or *The Dead Sea Scrolls*, the book darts from subject to subject and reveals the freest play of Wilson's imagination. The story goes that Wilson once visited Allen Tate in the South, put his bags down on the porch, and demanded, "Now where are the sharecroppers?" William Barrett, the reporter of this anecdote, also found that Wilson "would see only what he wanted to look at; his mind moved amid the words of some piece he was projecting and any perception could register only as it fell in line with what he might come to write."[11] *Upstate*'s pages of impressions overturn this otherwise shrewd and incisive observation: their variety and sense of wonder about the lives of ordinary Americans make this book Wilson's least insistent and most generous look at national life. A reflection rather than an investigation, it draws on Wilson's best sympathies as well as on some of his most irritable opinions.

The house, the town, and the observer's consciousness are subtly intertwined in this book about connections and sharing. Wilson opens his consciousness to the stories of relatives long forgotten, to new friends, to his physical environment. Although the six opening chapters present his cast of characters and study the history of the house in a conventional way, the heart of the book is 300 pages of journal material that weaves impressions together in a loose, informal, associational way. Books and people, landscapes and interiors all play a part in this remembrance of things past and encounter with things present. Wilson's technique has certain Proustian qualities—especially a passionate involvement with the details and texture of the physical world. The book's moral center is also Proustian: the conviction that preserving one's impressions of lives and of a place constitutes a way of making sense of the world.

The region around Talcottville is a moral force in the book. Like an old-fashioned scene painter, Wilson renders his environs in awesome and sublime terms. He applies language as a romantic painter applies color and light to make a landscape dramatic. Big trees "give the country its unsuppressible strength." There is also "the relatively primitive relation of people to the environment they live in. Nobler country here, which, I think, has made nobler people. It is part of the foundation of my whole life." Elsewhere "the dignity and beauty of the country" cause him to think of the "free and flourishing" settlers and "their human relationships and labors against the non-human grandeur of the setting." When he talks about the run-down condition of his house, he says that he "must bring it up again to the countryside." Almost like a character in a Wordsworth poem, he shows the way that he derives his sentiment of being from the perdurable qualities of the natural world.

The other aspect of the physical world is the stone house. At the beginning of the book, Wilson describes the whole process of reacquainting himself with the place from the vantage point of 1969. This opening is hardly different in tone from the 1930s essay in *The American Earthquake*: the author is sitting amid the broken pieces of the past; he tells us, just as the 1930s narrator did, that "all the old ghosts are gone." But if that were really so—emotional fact rather than posture—we would not soon learn about family and friends and their relation to the rooms and things that surround Wilson. His purpose in going to Talcottville and in writing the book was to galvanize this house, to charge it with significance. He does this by summoning up historical facts and physical details that make the place an intelligible link with the past and a center of order and harmony. He recalls that funeral services for George Washington were held here, that the line between Lewis and Oneida counties was drawn at a meeting in the house, that the china closet was once the village post office. Wilson, of course, is quite distant from the antiquarian or historical-monument attitude of those antique collectors and civic leaders who harbor a passion for charm. Like many nineteenth- and twentieth-century artists, he is using a house to shore up his own belief in order and beauty.[12] Here, he seems to say, is a place that can be made to live again and give security and comfort to the self. Although there is a tincture of aristocratic romanticism in his attitude toward his house—Wilson the gentleman in the big house surveying his neighbors from the porch—there is an even more powerful desire to find order and pattern in the world. In one impression Wilson conveys this desire by writing of "the well-knit house with its gratuitous elegance of front door and fireplaces—human art in the selection of view and the designing of the windows to frame it. My tendency is to feel that the view is a series of pictures and panels, that it is actually due to the intention of the builder." Wilson the critic has discovered and taken pleasure in the fusion of natural and man-made just as he took pleasure in the harmonious fusions of Proust and Joyce in *Axel's Castle*. The house becomes a kind of triumph of human imagination, a symbol that one can also live in. In a literary sense it represents the resolution of the conflict between the castle and human life.

Wilson's reverence for the order of his castle soon becomes a reverence for the people connected with it. He is sustained and energized not by a private isolated fantasy but by these people. One woman, Wilson's cousin Dorothy Reed Mendenhall, becomes a representative of Wilson's "nobler people." She is also one of his finest portraits of women, an expression of all that is most generous, observant, and sensitive in his nature. Cousin Dorothy, who is on the scene in the pages of *Upstate*, is Wilson's way of coming to terms with the modern woman as professional and intellectual.

After the spite and venom in the portrait of Judith, and the aggression discharged in his *Hecate County* portraits, Wilson now creates a woman who combines great stature as a physician with warmth, charm, personal stability, and a capacity for self-sacrifice. No Victorian paragon, Dorothy is described in her rebellion against a conventional and irresponsible mother. From early womanhood on, she is shown as having a healthy desire to break out of upper-class parochialism and leave her imprint on life. No conventional liberated woman, she is "unlike the much ridiculed type of the woman's rights champion." Like many struggling professional women in the early part of the century, she is presented as having an old-fashioned "high seriousness" and devotion to public service. Here we see Wilson enriching the portrait with ideas that he first used in his piece on Jane Addams, in this case a mediation between Dorothy's world of privilege as a member of an affluent family and her years of arduous work as a gynecologist. The medical profession, where she at first met ridicule and resistance, gave her the straightforward, unflinching attitude toward reality that Wilson has always championed, whether in the life of Marx, Lenin, or Jane Addams. Being able to see things steadily and whole—as they are in all their complexity and intractability—is the high virtue of *Finland Station's* successful men—and of Dorothy. Like Wilson himself Dorothy took a certain pride in encountering physical reality. She wrote about medical problems without restraint and with a personal candor uncharacteristic of her times, just as Wilson presented the uglier aspects of sex in *Hecate*

County. Among the people of *Upstate,* she becomes an exemplar of stead-fastness and realism, a woman Wilson can share feelings with.

While at Talcottville Wilson developed a friendship with Mary Pco-lar, a vivacious and intelligent Hungarian-American woman who lived in the area and who taught him her language. This relationship brought out a side of his character that had seemed dormant in the stormy years when he was attacking institutions and injustices. Wilson becomes Ödön Bácsi—Uncle Edmund, the honorary Hungarian, partygoer, friendly visitor, and solicitous older man. His interest in Mary's wel-fare—her family, jobs, college courses—is a way in which he has worked through the distanced attitude of *Hecate County* and gone beyond, not to another "investigation" of the Iroquois or Israelis, but to a friendship that enriches his work in its own subtle way. The pages of *Upstate* are deepened by something beyond intellectual mastery and the usual enthusiasm for discovering. Wilson has abandoned the role of the reporter—which inevitably involved him in watching the spectacle of human beings—in favor of the role of the memoirist and recounter of moments of friendly exchange. He sheds the rigors of his investigative style and puts on a summer mood—gentle, informal, undemanding.

These moments of relaxation and easy friendship come frequently but do not by any means suffuse the whole book. Wilson is no serene old man of a Wordsworth meditation, and his upstate story is punctu-ated by testy outbursts against American life. The book contains, for example, the story of Wilson's battle with the local motorcycle gang, and threaded throughout is also a series of pessimistic and none too rea-sonable attacks on his fellow citizens. The ugliest aspect of this can be seen as he observes the people in a thruway cafeteria near Lily Dale. They "seemed very low grade," bred down like so many specimens who, he seems to imply, are not the products of his idiotic eugenic ideas.

Elsewhere, however, there is a certain forthright, sad modulation of tone as he describes his own disillusionment. There is no nastiness or delight as he admits to feeling "a boredom with and even a scorn for the human race." Despite the small triumphs over modern chaos in the por-trait of Dorothy, despite the breakthroughs and literary resolutions of conflict, despite the galvanizing of the old house into life, there is an abiding sense of loss and irrepressible resentment in the book. The malaise of *The American Earthquake* has never completely cleared up. As he reads the newspapers, he claims that he has learned "not to hate the fools I read about." We, of course, do not believe this. It is the age of Nixon and Agnew—figures "hardly superior to the mediocrities that preside over the Soviet Union"—and Wilson is still in search of the headquarters of humanity. He portrays himself as the old man who knows that he must try to be calm as he sees his vision receding from the American scene. His outbursts in this book are not among his best, yet they should remind us that he has kept faith with his 1930s ideals and has not abandoned America for private concerns.

The better pessimistic musings in the book are free of bluster and prejudice. They simply express doubt and fear about human destiny. He comes to feel "the constant flow and perishable character, rather than the constant renewal and hope, of everything on earth." But while the attitude of staunch resistance seems gone, in its place there is a modest, qualified attitude toward the facts of human achievement. Ending in doubt—visiting great houses like Clarke-Hyde Hall that are now abandoned—he does not give way to any majestic elegy, any celebration of the past that would make him into the familiar nostalgic Tory. His purpose in this book has been to show how he took a part in a rational and humane way of life. His classic sense of limitations and his distaste for romantic trumpetings can be seen in his awkward, qualified ending: "I am glad to have had some share in some of the better aspects of the life of this planet and of northern New York."

Chapter Eight
A Wilson Portrait Gallery: The Public Sharer

Wilson's literary code of honor—that writers and other creative thinkers and actors must master and transform their limiting circumstances and must resist the demoralizing and cheapening tendencies of their times—is a theme that runs through all his work. Although panic, depression, and the corruptions and temptations of easier ways of life assail the creative person—and although much of Wilson's work studies frustration and submission—there is hope to be found in the artist's resistance and stubbornness. Wilson's excellence as well as his limitations can be seen in his half-century campaign of resistance against orthodox communism, patriotism, academic scholarship, state incursion, religion and conventional morality, obscurity in art, and the American good life. Hardly a cherished value or institution has escaped the cross-questioning of this mind in its pursuit of clarity, excellence, and progress.

The pursuit of these goals carries with it a number of limitations. As a critic of twentieth-century literature and thought, Wilson has made a point of resisting radically negative minds. Kafka's ambivalence, the tragic entrapment of his characters, and the confusion of their goals, for example, are at odds with a mind that has searched for and found possibilities in authors and societies. On the one hand, for a critic of modern art, Wilson has shown a strange lack of interest in the destructive element and the antiheroic: visions of an absurd universe and studies of nihilistic characters either chill or disgust him. On the other hand, his skepticism and irony have kept him at a distance from spiritual values and metaphysical beliefs that have nurtured many of the twentieth century's great minds. When Yeats and Eliot and Lawrence write about modern life and literature, they bring to it a spiritual intensity that Wilson seems immunized against. And finally, there is what Norman Podhoretz has identified as Wilson's limitations of character,[1] a hardness and narrowness that can be seen in his all too cool and clear views on eugenics, sex, and women. Whether a result of his patrician education or a legacy from his public-spirited but high-handed father, such attitudes constitute a real deficiency in a writer whose subject has often been human progress; they give an ugly coloration to an important book like *A Piece of My Mind*, and they taint *Hecate County* and *Upstate*. In cultivating the ethos of resistance and endurance, Wilson sometimes lapses into a kind of intellectual and emotional Darwinism as he dismisses the unfit from his vision of the "better aspects of life on this planet."

Once understood, however, these limitations should not prevent the reader from appreciating Wilson's power to seek out, delineate, and sympathize with men and women who have furthered human understanding through art and action. The headquarters of humanity—once a dream of humane relationships in "A Preface to Persius," later a vision of revolution in *To the Finland Station*, and finally a vision of the artist as resister—remains as a location in Wilson's writing. In this headquarters are mounted the portraits of humanists and artists, the great and the minor: Proust, Lenin, Mr. Rolphe, Major Eatherly, Indian leaders, Essene Jews, labor organizers.

The careers of three people distill the essence of Wilson's vision; their lives are the subjects of three portraits that Wilson wrote after the Second World War. As he describes Edna Millay the poet, George Santayana the philosopher, and Oliver Wendell Holmes the jurist, he shares their insight into art and thought and worldly action at the same time that he builds his own positions.[2]

"Edna St. Vincent Millay" serves as an epilogue to *The Shores of Light*, an official farewell to a major figure of the twenties and thirties. The final look at Edna's story—her great lyric talent and her struggle to overcome a neurotic nature—is extraordinarily tender, even a bit indulgent. It is essentially a personal response to the artist's travail. The story of his love for Edna is a good deal clearer than it was in *I Thought of Daisy*, and her charm and brilliance are much more understandable. This is to say, finally, that Wilson's gifts as a portraitist are greater than his talents as a narrator in fiction. Here the frantic, blurred Rita is replaced by the beautiful Edna.

One of the ways that Wilson brings Edna to life is by telling his own story. This time, however, it is dependent on succinct and controlled observations that are more memorable than the pages of talk in the novel. A part of himself is detached and placed in every scene. Wilson begins with his discovery of Edna's work and the ardor he felt when he used to chant "To Love Impuissant" in the shower. He soon meets and falls in love with the blazing poetess, and instead of *Daisy*'s musings, we get a more restrained Wilson remembering how Frank Crowninshield, the editor of *Vanity Fair*, was vexed because both of his assistants—Wilson and John Peale Bishop—were in love with the same brilliant contributor. Later, when Wilson goes to Cape Cod to visit Edna and her family, he proposes marriage. There are no rhapsodic passages here either; Wilson simply observes that proposals were evidently not a source of great excitement to Edna. He tells us that on another occasion he assisted her by transcribing lines of her dictated poetry on the typewriter—while drinking bathtub gin: "This exhilarating bitter liquor has always kept for me a certain glamour that others have not acquired." The offhandedness of this is more affecting than a page of effusions. Even when Wilson breaks down and describes his feelings, he refuses "to go back to that old state of mind." This distance from pain—with its wit, excitement, and sense of proportion—prevents him from damaging his subject matter.

The controlled but personal response is especially appropriate to the theme of the portrait: the real leap forward in Wilson's writing is seen as he describes Edna not in terms of weakness and wounds, but in terms of mastery. The essay is not about a neurotic woman but about a figure who can

> identify herself with more general human experience and stand forth as a spokesman for the human spirit, announcing its predicaments, its vicissitudes, but, as a master of human expression, by the splendor of expression itself, putting herself beyond human embarrassments and common oppressions and panics. This is man who surveys himself and the world in which he moves, not the beast that scurries and suffers.

In emphasizing the mastery rather than the vulnerability of the poet's condition, Wilson does not abandon his concern for the painful circumstances that are a part of creation. Instead he devises another metaphor to convey the poetic career: "The Shores of Light"—the title of the entire volume—refers to a passage from Virgil in which plants reach upward to the light. Wilson remarks that in a poem of his own written in 1928 he used the image to describe Edna's groping from the underworld of suffering. Edna's aspiration is further described and given dignity by Wilson's likening of her life to literature itself—austere, distanced, and condensed. The woman who was once the subject of a nebulous portrait in *Daisy* has now become the epitome of creative mastery.

It should be recognized, however, that the portrait involves an alteration of the initial reactions that Wilson had when he met Edna again in the late 1940s. The beauty of the piece comes from the blending of lies about responses and the selection of telling details. Readers of *The Forties* are not likely to forget Wilson's standoffish attitude toward the deteriorated friend of his youth. The journal writer who was glad to have avoided Edna's fate—and was none too generous in his observations about the emotionally tormented poetess—is very different from the writer who warmed to his subject in *The Shores of Light* and went beyond his petty insights about Edna's weakness to a truer, though less factually accurate, view of the poet's struggle and achievement. The Edna of the the volume's epilogue is a vibrant and fully realized woman artist, not a mere wrecked talent.

One of the most carefully crafted late portraits of the man of ideas, Wilson's account of his meeting with Santayana in *Europe Without Baedeker* (1947), presents a different kind of mastery: the serene, mocking, ironic command of Santayana becomes an exemplary way of living as a thinker. Wilson describes a position not unlike the one he assumes in *Upstate*, the detached man who is nevertheless not alone because he continues his dialogue with the world. It is an engaged kind of detachment, a possession of worldly knowledge without the torment that is obvious in the portrait of Edna. The resolution of conflict described in the portrait is Wilson's way of breaking out of the artist's destiny into a higher, more civilized form of living—something that he outlined vaguely in the dream synthesis of *Axel's Castle*.

In the portrait, Wilson uses his subject's views and nature as a way of depositing and tallying his own mature views about the situation of the thinker. Santayana, like Wilson, is a passionate communicator who is paradoxically living at a distance from other individuals. Like the Wilson who traveled and talked and listened with such seriousness of purpose, Santayana is "the sage who has made it his business to meet and to reflect on all kinds of men and who will talk about the purpose and practice of life with anyone who likes to discuss them—as with me, whom he didn't know from Adam—since these were matters which concern us all." In describing Santayana's work, Wilson also uses a highly selective, if not distorted, approach to a very abstract thinker. The philosopher who wrote volumes on essences and other "realms of being" is made to sound like Wilson himself: "A man in the world who was trying to make some sense of it as you were." While perhaps true in some general sense, this portrait is hardly characteristic of one of American thought's most majestic and removed figures; what the description does do is reveal something of Wilson's hope for the man of ideas. It is further developed as he celebrates Santayana's enthusiasm for others' opinions. The aged philosopher, like Wilson in *A Piece of My Mind* and *Upstate*, is never completely detached from the world: "He still loves to share in its thoughts, to try on its points of view. He has made it his business to extend himself into every kind of human consciousness with which he can establish contact, and he reposes on his shabby chaise lounge like a monad in the universal mind." This last striking image— humanized by the physical detail and yet generalized—distills what Wilson sought in his writings that deal with ideas. Rooted in the ordinary world—much like Santayana's idea that spiritual ideals proceed from our naturalistic condition—Wilson's career as a thinker, as a student of socialism or religion or the ideas in literature, is an attempt to reach beyond his immediate environment and touch the filaments of very different minds. As Wilson wrote, he sought not only subjects for books but also the companionship and encouragement of the symbolists or Marx or the Essenes. By making it "his business to extend himself into every kind of human consciousness," he not only broke down some of the isolation that he began with but also made himself a vigorous and enthusiastic sharer who never wrote himself into a dead end and never experienced the profound isolation of the writer who is alone with his obsessions. Like the Santayana he describes, Wilson is the most social of writers: "Nor is he really alone in the sense that the ordinary person would be. He is still in the world of men, conversing with them through reading and writing, a section of the human plasm that, insulated by convent walls and by exceptional resistances of character, still registers the remotest tremors." If the "convent walls" of the Blue Nuns are changed to Wilson's own distance from the world, the apposition between the two men is nearly perfect—a creative critic's way of exploring his own position by looking at another man.

Another philosophic mind, that of Oliver Wendell Holmes Jr. the jurist and social thinker, provides Wilson with the opportunity to reveal a side of himself. Lacking Santayana's geniality, Holmes endures and triumphs through an essentially negative discipline of the self—a lifelong campaign against cant, crusades, and moral ideals. The Holmes portrait, the final chapter in *Patriotic Gore*, is a presentation of a hero as naysayer in a time of yea-saying. While many men and women who felt the pressure of the Civil War responded by lining up ideologically and crusading for violence by adopting the vocabulary of Calvinism, Holmes was unconverted to the Union cause by his near death on the battlefield. Another of Wilson's unconverts, he denied God and with Him all social illusions about righteousness and justice. Wilson portrays the ways in which this "everlasting no" shaped one of the most remarkably resistant careers of the century. Holmes, like some twentieth-century *philosophe,* said no to the enthusiasms of his contemporaries: to the idea of absolute morality, to abstract notions of social justice, to the pieties of big business and the political left. The man who was educated decisively on the battlefield—who concluded from the spectacle of human misery that social order rests on the deaths of men—cast a cold eye on ideologies at the same time that he grimly recognized the overriding significance of the power drive in human affairs.

Wilson's presentation of this anti-idealistic career is the occasion for revealing his own resistance to empires and social ideals as well as an opportunity to draw back from Holmes's granitelike devotion to rationalist principles. This chapter, unlike Wilson's more pugnacious attacks on illogical institutions, celebrates Holmes's triumph over fanaticism while at the same time expressing a chilled response to the rational mind and its wrecking operations. Holmes is "a tough character, purposive, disciplined and not a little hard." Wilson describes him as selfish, vain, and thoughtless of others. But for all Holmes's distrust of institutions, he put his life at the service of the nation-state—and left his personal estate to the government. Wilson has assembled within this portrait his own traits as a public thinker, probity, professionalism, and devotion to larger causes. But he sets himself apart from his subject by reminding the reader of the human cost of high rational achievement, and in so doing he enumerates his own mistakes.

In working as a portraitist and creative writer, a literary critic, a thinker reflecting on his age and other times, and a journalist and social critic, Wilson shared the ideas of many people. The development of his career is much like that of Joseph Conrad's young protagonist in "The Secret Sharer." Conrad's young captain discovers how to master his craft and command his ship as a result of his encounter with a double—a secret sharer whose life and crises become a way for the captain to learn about himself—and Wilson found public sharers of his own fate, from the early symbolists to the Marxists to the people in *Upstate.* He conducted his development as a writer by publicly adopting and rejecting the ideas of other men and women in order to shape his own durable, commanding literary self. But while his particular kind of creativity involved sharing, it was always complicated by his aloof nature. It became a matter of conflicts: social and political engagement versus isolation, genial communion versus angry or ironic withdrawal. These con-

flicts persisted until the end of his life, but he worked to resolve them—
to find some higher synthesis, to create a reconciliation of opposites by
writing about men and women whose careers represent a successful balancing of ideas and emotions and an attainment of an identity beyond
that of class and temperament. In Edna Millay, for instance, he created a
model of the heroic artist who "stands forth" in the name of the human
spirit and demonstrates a kind of literary courage that is all the more
important because it is so much a victory over neurotic personality.
With Oliver Wendell Holmes, Wilson presents a figure whose discontent with his own situation as a lawyer made him reach out for generalizations about the social condition of humanity that are far beyond the
purview of the legalistic mind. Santayana—at once participant and sovereign self—represents the most successful negotiation between
impulses and ideas. In his best books, and even sometimes in his weak-
est, Wilson strives to make himself worthy of the phrase that he used to
describe Santayana: "a monad in the universal mind."

Notes and References

Introduction

1. See Janet Groth and David Castronovo, eds., *From the Uncollected Edmund Wilson* (Athens: Ohio University Press, 1995). Ohio University Press is reprinting *The Wound and the Bow*.

2. Frank Kermode, *Puzzles and Epiphanies* (London: Routledge & Kegan Paul, 1962), p. 57.

3. Groth and Castronovo, *From the Uncollected*, p. 242.

4. *Patriotic Gore: Studies in the Literature of the American Civil War* (New York: Oxford University Press, 1962).

5. For the references to Powell and Ade, see *The Bit between My Teeth: A Literary Chronicle of 1950–1965* (New York: Farrar, Straus & Giroux, 1965).

6. Obituary by Michael Norman, *New York Times,* Oct. 25, 1996, section A, p. 33.

7. Groth and Castronovo, *From the Uncollected,* pp. 73–75.

8. Hubert Butler, *"Two Critics" in Independent Spirit* (New York: Farrar, Straus & Giroux, 1996), pp. 271–81.

9. Amis and Wilson are covered in *The Bit between My Teeth.*

10. Groth and Castronovo, *From The Uncollected,* p. 252.

11. Isaiah Berlin's observation is reported by Edel in *The Fifties: From the Notebooks and Diaries of the Period* (edited and introduced by Leon Edel. New York: Farrar, Straus & Giroux, 1986), p. 100.

12. See chapter 6 of this volume.

13. Michel de Montaigne, "On Some Verses of Virgil," in *The Complete Essays of Montaigne* (Stanford: Stanford University Press, 1976), Book III, pp. 638–85.

Chapter One

1. Wilson's notebooks are a detailed recording of his impressions of himself, books and ideas in his life, people, and events. Leon Edel, Wilson's literary executor for years, edited and introduced *The Twenties, The Thirties, The Forties,* and *The Fifties;* Lewis Dabney edited *The Sixties.* Wilson himself saw the publication of an earlier volume concerned with his youth, *A Prelude: Landscapes, Characters and Conversations from the Earlier Years of My Life* (New York: Farrar, Straus & Giroux, 1967). Edel reminds us that Wilson did not want to "cut corners," that he wanted the notebooks—with many of their shortsighted perceptions and other weaknesses—to stand beside his other works. Readers who go through them will find a rich storehouse of experiences; they will also find a good deal of jotting and verbal doodling, random impressions, and arch

149

cocktail conversation. But all together these notebooks are invaluable source material for piecing together Wilson's life and for understanding the tenor of his mind. In addition to these, Wilson has left highly crafted portraits of friends, teachers, and family in his major works.

2. See Sherman Paul, *Edmund Wilson: A Study of Literary Vocation in Our Time* (Urbana: University of Illinois Press, 1965). This study, which is more concerned with Wilson's intellectual positions than with analysis of his works, emphasizes the episode with the rich boy and sees it as a central experience.

3. Wilson's *Letters on Literature and Politics, 1912–1973* ed. Elena Wilson (New York: Farrar, Straus & Giroux, 1977) are, from the first pages written by the Hill School boy, a monument to a life of reading and writing. Large sections of this volume are devoted to correspondence about his own works; almost every letter directly or indirectly discusses printed words.

4. See Christian Gauss, "Edmund Wilson: The Campus and *The Nassau 'Lit,'*" *The Princeton University Library Chronicle* 5, no. 2 (February 1944): pp. 41–50.

5. See the essay on Whipple and Princeton in *Classics and Commercials: A Literary Chronicle of the Forties* (New York: Farrar, Straus, 1950; reprint, New York: Vintage Books, 1962).

6. Stanley Edgar Hyman, a critic with little admiration for Wilson, reports this in *The Armed Vision* (New York: Knopf, 1948), p. 37.

7. For a full treatment of Gauss, see the opening chapter of *The Shores of Light* (New York: Farrar, Straus & Young, 1952; reprint, New York: Vintage Books, 1962; paper reprint, Boston: Northeastern University Press, 1985).

8. Edel's remarks on Wilson's sex life are in the introduction to *The Twenties*, pp. xxvi–xxvii, and the introduction to *The Thirties*, p. xxviii.

9. For a treatment of Wilson as a "crotchety old man," see especially Leonard Kriegel, *Edmund Wilson* (Carbondale: Southern Illinois Press, 1971), pp. 118–20. Kriegel wonders why Wilson is heated up about what everyone knows; he also thinks that the book is a dead end as a protest.

10. For an affectionate and reverent portrait of Wilson in his later life, see Alfred Kazin, "The Great Anachronism: A View from the Sixties," in John Wain, ed., *Edmund Wilson: The Man and His Work* (New York: New York University Press, 1978), pp. 11–27.

11. Some interesting aspects of social life in Talcottville and Wilson's habits are to be found in Richard Hauer Costa, *Edmund Wilson: Our Neighbor from Talcottville* (Syracuse, N.Y.: Syracuse University Press, 1980).

12. See Richard David Ramsay, *Edmund Wilson: A Bibliography* (New York: D. Lewis, 1971). This book devotes more than 300 pages to listing Wilson's works.

Chapter Two

1. On Wilson's intense concern for his reader, see Alfred Kazin, *On Native Grounds* (New York: Reynal and Hitchcock, 1942), pp. 450–51.

2.   Among those who have discussed Wilson's lack of original ideas in his literary criticism, see Kazin, *On Native Grounds,* pp. 449, 451; Warner Berthoff, "Edmund Wilson," in *American Writers* (New York: Charles Scribner's Sons, 1974) vol. 4, pp. 440–42; and Hyman, *The Armed Vision.* Kazin's remarks are in a larger context of praise for a "mediator" rather than a great leader. Berthoff's discussion of Wilson's "airless" mind and his cool knowingness—along with an analysis of his derivative ideas—is exceedingly valuable reading, but it fails to convey Wilson's excited responses to literature; it sees a great critic's limitations as not unlike those of the static and essentially rigid class of professionals to which his father belonged. Hyman's criticism—omitted from the 1955 edition of his book—is savage, often witty, and very often irresponsible. He makes Wilson sound like a "translator" of others' works and ideas; ad hominem attacks abound here, but the essay is essential for an understanding of the scholarly mentality that dismisses Wilson as a popularizer.

3.   For a brilliant consideration of Wilson's ambivalence, see Frank Kermode, *Puzzles and Epiphanies: Essays and Reviews 1958–1961* (London: Routledge & Kegan Paul, 1962), especially p. 59.

4.   Some critics have concluded from this response that Wilson has difficulty analyzing and appreciating symbolist poetry—and poetry in general. Hyman says Wilson doesn't have much sensitivity to verse. Matthew Josephson feels Wilson is out of sympathy with some symbolists (*Saturday Review,* March 7, 1931, p. 642); F. O. Matthiessen sees many inaccuracies of interpretation in *The Responsibilities of the Critic* (New York: Oxford University Press, 1952), pp. 159–61.

5.   Berthoff, p. 443.

6.   For a good discussion of writers and critics who equate social significance with literary significance, see William Van O'Connor, *An Age of Criticism* (Chicago: Regnery, 1952), pp. 110–32.

7.   See O'Connor, p. 127, and Hyman, p. 34.

8.   See Lionel Trilling, "Art and Neurosis," *The Liberal Imagination* (New York: Viking, 1950), pp. 155–75. For a representative sampling of those who feel Wilson is not successful, see Charles Frank, *Edmund Wilson* (New York: Twayne, 1970), pp. 42–48 (Frank uses the term "psychobiography" as a negative label), and Delmore Schwartz, "The Writing of Edmund Wilson," *Accent,* 2 (Spring 1942): pp. 177–86. Schwartz picks apart Wilson's idea of the wound in Sophocles.

9.   Leonard Kriegel joins those who are critical of Wilson's emphasis on wounds. In reading the Casanova essay, however, he fails to recognize Wilson's purpose—to show how a minor writer and personage struggles.

Chapter Three

1.   Murray Kempton has made a similar point in his superb chapter dealing with Wilson's social and political journalism and other writers'

responses to the thirties and the siren call of Marxist ideology; he reminds us that Wilson's revolt against American materialism "had been born in the twenties and not in the depression." Kempton is especially sensitive to the independent quality of Wilson's protest. See "The Social Muse," in Kempton's *Part of Our Time: Some Ruins and Monuments of the Thirties* (New York: Simon & Schuster, 1955), pp. 105–51.

2. See Leonard Kriegel, p. 36. He refers to Wilson's bitter, ironic vision and the thirties journalism as a charting of "the geography of American humiliation." In his treatment of the journalism, Kriegel does not integrate the culture and art with the social upheavals; instead he surveys Wilson's scenes of thirties disaster.

3. The best treatment of Wilson's art of reporting is contained in a few impressionistic pages by Alfred Kazin; he argues that Wilson's temperament and intense concentration account for the excitement of his prose. See "Edmund Wilson on the Thirties," in Kazin's *Contemporaries* (Boston: Little, Brown, 1962), pp. 405–11.

4. Frank, p. 111.

5. Paul, p. 32.

6. Charles Frank argues that Wilson uses "fictionalized fact" and "ironic contrasts" in his journalism. His startling conclusion about Wilson's technique—that the journalism should be seen as an "anatomy" of society and contemporary attitudes—is not reinforced with good comparisons between some anatomy (say a seventeenth-century work that criticizes society) and Wilson's work.

7. Norman Podhoretz, in his searching essay "Edmund Wilson: Then and Now," *Doings and Undoings* (New York: Farrar, Straus, 1964), pp. 46–47, thinks Wilson is too critical of trashy aspects in the work of the "Boys." Podhoretz regards this as another of Wilson's simplifications of experience, a failure to understand the problematic world the writer must deal with.

Chapter Four

1. Brief references to *Finland Station*'s fictional qualities can be found in Marshall Berman's review of the 1971 reprint in the *New York Times Book Review*, August 20, 1972, p. 1; C. O. Cleveland's review in *Commonweal* 33 (October 25, 1940): p. 32; and Kriegel, p. 58.

2. Although Wilson evaluates the dialectic—and refuses to accept it as an ironclad way of interpreting history—he accepts his "actors' " belief in it to the extent that he finds their work coherent and based on noble aspirations and solid reasoning. He rejects the theological worship of the method, however.

3. A suggestive treatment of history and Marxism can be found in Reinhold Niebuhr's review "The Goddess of History," *Nation* 151 (September 24, 1940): pp. 274, 276.

4. Hyman infers from this that Wilson reduces Marxism to carbuncles.

5. Paul Fussell, *Abroad* (New York: Oxford University Press, 1980), pp. 15–24.

6. Malcolm Cowley, "From the Finland Station," *New Republic* 103 (October 7, 1940): p. 480.

7. Kriegel, p. 56.

8. Marshall Berman observes that Wilson's portrait of Lenin is an unintentional indictment.

Chapter Five

1. On Rita and Edna, see Paul, pp. 55–56. See also chapter 8 of this volume.

2. Edna evidently didn't like her portrait in *Daisy* and asked him not to publish the book; see Frank, pp. 194–95.

3. On origins of Grosbeake, see *Letters,* p. 176.

4. Floyd Dell, *Intellectual Vagabondage* (New York: Doran 1926), p. 205.

5. For two criticisms that focus on fragmentation—and are out of sympathy with Wilson's vision—see Kriegel, pp. 75–78, and Diana Trilling, *Reviewing the Forties* (New York: Harcourt Brace Jovanovich, 1978), pp. 150–54.

6. Paul, p. 165.

7. Paul, p. 153.

8. For Wilson's interest in magic—he often gave performances for family and friends while fortified with liquor—see *Letters,* p. 574.

9. Frank, p. 152.

10. Diana Trilling, pp. 153–54.

11. On some of the legal proceedings and testimony, see the afterword to *Memoirs of Hecate County* (Boston: Nonpareil, 1980), pp. 449–52.

12. Vladimir Nabokov wrote Wilson a letter with a similar response to *Hecate's* sensual women: "I should have as soon tried to open a sardine can with my penis. The result is remarkably chaste, despite the frankness."

13. Yvor Winters, *Primitivism and Decadence* (New York: Haskell House, 1937), pp. 49–52.

14. Irving Howe, "The Culture of Modernism," in *Decline of the New* (New York: Harcourt Brace and World, 1970), p. 16.

Chapter Six

1. On Wilson's disenchantment with communism during the *Finland Station* period, see Kriegel, pp. 56, 66.

2. Irving Howe, *A World More Attractive: A View of Modern Literature and Politics* (New York: Horizon Press,1963), p. 303.

3. Kenneth Lynn, "The Right to Secede from History," *New Republic* 146 (June 25, 1962): p. 21.

4. See *Letters on Literature and Politics,* pp. 608–23.

5. See, for example, Howe, pp. 306–7.

6. For a representative sampling of the best Marxist criticism as applied to style, see Georg Lukács and Christopher Caudwell in *Marxists on Literature,* ed. David Craig (Baltimore: Penguin, 1975).

7. Alfred Kazin rhapsodizes about *Patriotic Gore* in his *New York Jew,* pp. 376–80. Like a number of other critics, he tends to play down the importance of the angry tone and emphasize Wilson's deep understanding of people—especially the more attractive ones—and reverence for the American past.

8. For information on the play's reception, see Frank, pp. 92–93.

Chapter Seven

1. Paul describes this side of Wilson's art as "prophecy" and sums up its "message": "That man must persist and that art (in the most inclusive sense and always as the polar term for ideology) enables him to."

2. For a treatment of Wilson's "coarseness and confusion," see Berthoff pp. 437–39. Berthoff argues that Wilson does not understand the character of Kafka's mind; he also feels that Wilson is superficial in dealing with Kafka's weakness.

3. William Barrett, *Time of Need: Forms of Imagination in the Twentieth Century* (New York: Harper & Row, 1972), p. 239.

4. Leon Edel, foreword to *Israel and the Dead Sea Scrolls,* p. xii.

5. David Flusser, an important Hebraist, gives a favorable evaluation of Wilson's work; he regards the Scrolls book as "a turning point in the research of the history of religions." See Flusser, "Not Obliged to Any Religion" in John Wain, ed., *Edmund Wilson: The Man and His Work,* pp. 109–14.

6. Wilson's enthusiasm for Boris Pasternak takes the form of lengthy essays that analyze life-availing images in Pasternak's writing; both Wilson's thematic concern for endurance and his attention to conventional symbols can be seen in the essays in *The Bit between My Teeth;* for Nabokov's strangely textured prose there is much less understanding. On the question of Wilson's problematic relationship to modern literature after Proust and Joyce, see Richard Gilman, "Edmund Wilson, Then and Now," *New Republic,* June 2, 1966, pp. 23–28.

7. Sherman Paul's conviction that Wilson is of "a religious disposition" seems to miss the mark; time after time in his writing—from boyhood to old age—Wilson attacks group beliefs, and even personal communion with God. Wilson is, however, devoted to ideas of sacrifice and work for causes that are secularizations of Christian and Jewish teachings.

8. The story of Wilson's intense involvement with Jewish writing and culture can be followed on a personal level in *Letters,* especially in the time he took to describe his excitement to Alfred Kazin (pp. 523, 527, 528) and also to a friendly reader from New Jersey, Jacob Landau (especially pp. 471–74). Kazin was amused by Wilson's remark about Jewish history: "Once you really

get into it, you find there is no easy way of getting out again." Landau became a kind of literary friend and fellow enthusiast and gave Wilson bits of informa- tion—and became another personal link with a tradition. The best treatment of Wilson and Jewish culture, an essay by Mark Krupnick, will soon appear in a volume published by Princeton University Press.

9. A modern scholarly and humanistic appraisal of eugenics can be found in Allen Chase, *The Legacy of Malthus* (New York: Knopf, 1977).

10. Leonard Kriegel makes a case for Wilson's "retreat" from involve- ment and the American scene. See Kriegel, chapters 4 and 5.

11. William Barrett, *The Truants: Adventures among the Intellectuals* (Gar- den City, N.Y.: Anchor Doubleday, 1982), p. 61.

12. On the country house in modern English literature, see Richard Gill, *Happy Rural Seat* (New Haven: Yale University Press, 1972). Wilson's old stone house, it should be noted, is a place that has been "galvanized" into life. His relationship to it is more problematic than that of writers who saw the country house as a principle of coherence and tradition. In *Upstate* Wilson pro- gressed from a dispirited attitude to guarded reverence to a kind of tragic resig- nation; this is far different from, say, Evelyn Waugh's romanticism in *Brideshead Revisited,* a novel for which Wilson had little regard (see *Classics and Commercials,* pp. 300–302).

Chapter Eight

1. Podhoretz, p. 37.
2. See Lynn, p. 23, on Wilson's "projecting" in the portrait of Holmes.

Bibliography

PRIMARY WORKS

The Undertaker's Garland. In collaboration with John Peale Bishop. New York: Knopf, 1922.

Discordant Encounters: Plays and Dialogues. New York: Boni, 1926.

I Thought of Daisy. New York: Scribners, 1929; reprint, New York: Farrar, Straus & Young, 1953; reprint, New York: Ballantine, 1953; reprint, New York: Penguin, 1963; New York: Farrar, Straus & Giroux, 1967.

Poets, Farewell! New York: Scribners, 1929.

Axel's Castle: A Study in the Imaginative Literature of 1870 to 1930. New York: Scribners, 1931; reprint, paper, New York: Norton, 1984; reprint, New York: Modern Library, 1996.

The American Jitters: A Year of the Slump. New York: Scribners, 1932; reprint, North Stratford, N.H,: Ayer, 1980.

Travels in Two Democracies. New York: Harcourt Brace, 1936.

This Room and This Gin and These Sandwiches: Three Plays. New York: New Republic, 1937.

The Triple Thinkers: Ten Essays on Literature. New York: Harcourt Brace, 1938; reprint, New York: Oxford University Press, 1948; reprint, New York: Galaxy Books, Oxford University Press, 1963.

To the Finland Station: A Study in the Writing and Acting of History. New York: Harcourt, Brace, 1940; reprint, Garden City, N.Y.: Anchor Doubleday; reprint, with new introduction, New York: Macmillan, 1972; reprint, Cutchogue, N.Y.: Buccaneer Books, 1994; reprint, paper, New York: Farrar, Straus & Giroux, 1994.

The Boys in the Back Room: Notes on California Novelists. San Francisco: Colt, 1941; reprint, in *Classics and Commercials*. New York: Farrar, Straus, 1950.

The Wound and the Bow: Seven Studies in Literature. Boston: Houghton Mifflin, 1941; reprint, London: University Paperbacks, Methuen, 1961.

Notebooks of Night. San Francisco: Colt, 1942.

The Shock of Recognition: The Development of Literature in the United States Recorded by the Men Who Made It. Garden City, N.Y.: Doubleday Doran, 1943; reprint, New York: Grosset & Dunlap, 1955.

Memoirs of Hecate County. Garden City, N.Y.: Doubleday 1946; reprint, New York: L. C. Page, 1949; reprint, New York: Signet Books, New American Library, [date]; reprint, Boston: Nonpareil, 1980; reprint, paper, New York: Farrar, Straus, & Giroux, 1996.

Europe Without Baedeker: Sketches among the Ruins of Italy, Greece, and England.
    Garden City, N.Y.: Doubleday, 1947.
Classics and Commercials: A Literary Chronicle of the Forties. New York: Farrar,
    Straus, 1950; reprint, New York: Vintage Books, 1962.
The Little Blue Light: A Play in Three Acts. New York: Farrar, Straus, 1950.
The Shores of Light: A Literary Chronicle of the Twenties and Thirties. New York:
    Farrar, Straus & Young, 1952; reprint, New York: Vintage Books, 1962;
    reprint, paper, Boston: Northeastern University Press, 1985.
Eight Essays. Garden City, N.Y.: Doubleday, 1954.
Five Plays. New York: Farrar, Straus & Young, 1954.
The Scrolls from the Dead Sea. New York: Oxford University Press, 1955.
A Literary Chronicle: 1920–1950. Garden City, N.Y.: Doubleday, 1956.
A Piece of My Mind: Reflections at Sixty. New York: Farrar, Straus & Cudahy,
    1956; reprint, Garden City, N.Y.: Anchor Doubleday, 1958.
*Red, Black, Blond and Olive: Studies in Four Civilizations: Zuni, Haiti, Soviet Rus-
    sia, Israel.* New York: Oxford University Press, 1956.
The American Earthquake: A Documentary of the Twenties and Thirties. Garden City,
    N.Y.: Doubleday, 1958; reprint, New York: DaCapo, 1996.
Apologies to the Iroquois. New York: Farrar, Straus & Cudahy, 1960; reprint,
    paper, Syracuse: Syracuse University Press, 1992.
Night Thoughts. New York: Farrar, Straus & Cudahy, 1961.
Patriotic Gore: Studies in the Literature of the American Civil War. New York:
    Oxford University Press, 1962; reprint, paper, New York: Norton;
    reprint, Magnolia, Mass.: Peter Smith, 1995.
The Cold War and the Income Tax: A Protest. New York: Farrar, Straus & Cudahy,
    1963.
The Bit between My Teeth: A Literary Chronicle of 1950–1965. New York: Farrar,
    Straus & Giroux, 1965.
O Canada: An American's Notes on Canadian Culture. New York: Farrar, Straus &
    Giroux, 1965.
A Prelude: Landscapes, Characters and Conversations from the Earlier Years of My Life.
    New York: Farrar, Straus & Giroux, 1967.
Upstate: Records and Recollections of Northern New York. New York: Farrar, Straus &
    Giroux, 1971; reprint, Syracuse: Syracuse University Press, 1990.
A Window on Russia for the Use of Foreign Readers. New York: Farrar, Straus &
    Giroux, 1972.
The Devils and Canon Barham: Ten Essays on Poets, Novelists and Monsters. New
    York: Farrar, Straus & Giroux, 1973.
The Twenties: From Notebooks and Diaries of the Period. Edited by and with intro-
    duction by Leon Edel. New York: Farrar, Straus & Giroux, 1975.
Letters on Literature and Politics 1912–1972. Edited by Elena Wilson and with
    introduction by Daniel Aaron and foreword by Leon Edel. New York:
    Farrar, Straus & Giroux, 1977.

The Nabokov-Wilson Letters 1940–1971. Edited by Simon Karlinsky. New York: Harper Colophon Books, 1979.

The Thirties: From Notebooks and Diaries of the Period. Edited and with introduction by Leon Edel. New York: Farrar, Straus & Giroux, 1980.

The Forties: From Notebooks and Diaries of the Period. Edited and with introduction by Leon Edel. New York: Farrar, Straus & Giroux, 1983.

The Portable Edmund Wilson. Edited and with introduction by Lewis M. Dabney. New York: Penguin, 1983.

The Fifties: From Notebooks and Diaries of the Period. Edited and with introduction by Leon Edel. New York: Farrar, Straus & Giroux, 1986.

The Sixties: The Last Journal, 1960–1972. Edited and with introduction by Lewis Dabney. New York: Farrar, Straus & Giroux, 1993.

From the Uncollected Edmund Wilson. Edited and with introduction by Janet Groth and David Castronovo. Athens: University of Ohio Press, 1995.

SECONDARY SOURCES

Aaron, Daniel. *Writers on the Left: Episodes in American Literary Communism.* New York: Harcourt Brace, 1961.

Atlas, James. "The Last of the Big Time Polymaths," *New York Times Book Review,* July 28, 1985, p. 6.

Barrett, William. *Time of Need.* New York: Harper & Row, 1972.

Barrett, William. *The Truants: Adventure among the Intellectuals.* Garden City, N.Y.: Anchor Doubleday, 1982.

Berlin, Isaiah. "Edmund Wilson at Oxford." In *Encounters,* edited by Kai Erikson. New Haven: Yale University Press, 1989.

Berman, Marshall. Review of *To the Finland Station. New York Times Book Review,* August 20, 1972, p. 1.

Berman, Paul. "Edmund's Castle." *New Republic* 214 (June 3, 1996): 32–41

Berthoff, Warner. "Edmund Wilson." In *American Writers* (vol. 4, pp. 426–49). New York: Charles Scribner's Sons, 1974.

Butler, Hubert. *Independent Spirit.* New York: Farrar, Straus & Giroux, 1996.

Castronovo, David, and Anne Whitehouse. "Edmund Wilson's Citizen Reader," *Forward,* November 6, 1992, pp. 9, 14, 15.

Chandler, Raymond. *Selected Letters of Raymond Chandler.* Edited by Frank Mac-Shane. New York: Columbia University Press, 1981.

Cleveland, C. O. Review of *To the Finland Station. Commonweal* 33 (October 25, 1940): 32.

Commager, Henry Steele. "Myths, Morals and a House Divided." *New York Times Book Review,* April 29, 1962, pp. 1, 24.

Connolly, Cyril. "Edmund Wilson: An Appreciation." *Sunday Times (London),* June 18, 1972, p. 40.

Costa, Richard Hauer. *Edmund Wilson: Our Neighbor from Talcottville.* Syracuse, N.Y.: Syracuse University Press, 1980.

Cowley, Malcolm. "From the Finland Station." *New Republic* 103 (October 7, 1940): 478–80.

Craig, David, ed. *Marxists on Literature.* Baltimore: Penguin, 1975.

Dabney, Lewis. "Edmund Wilson, Jr.," *Sewanee Review* 103, no. 2 (April–June 1995): 198–230.

Dell, Floyd, *Intellectual Vagabondage.* New York: Doran, 1926.

Douglas, George. *Edmund Wilson's America.* Lexington: University of Kentucky Press, 1983.

Epstein, Jason. "The Man with Qualities." *New York Review of Books,* June 8, 1995, pp. 4, 6–7.

Epstein, Jason, "Wilson's Amerika," *New York Review of Books* 1 (November 28, 1983): 9–11.

Epstein, Joseph. "Bye, Bye Bunny." *Hudson Review* 47, no. 2 (Summer 1994): 235–48.

Frank, Charles. *Edmund Wilson.* New York: Twayne, 1970.

French, Philip, ed. *Three Honest Men: Edmund Wilson, F. R. Leavis, Lionel Trilling.* Manchester: Carcanet New Press, 1980.

Gauss, Christian. "Edmund Wilson, The Campus and *The Nassau 'Lit.'* " *The Princeton University Library Chronicle* 5 (February, 1944): 41–50.

Gilman, Richard. "Edmund Wilson, Then and Now." *New Republic* 34 (April 30, 1956): 13–16.

Gilman, Richard. "The Critic as Taxpayer." *New Republic,* 149 (November 30, 1963): 25–27.

Gilman, Richard. "Edmund's Castle." *New York Times Book Review,* December 31, 1995, p. 17.

Gross, John. Review of Castronovo's 1985 *Edmund Wilson. New York Times,* July 19, 1985, C19.

Groth, Janet. *Edmund Wilson: A Critic for Our Time.* Athens: Ohio University Press.

Hamilton, Ian. "The wound, the bow and the glory." *Times Literary Supplement,* October 27, 1995, pp. 4–5.

Howe, Irving. "Edmund Wilson and the Sea Slugs." In *A World More Attractive,* pp. 300-7. New York: Horizon Press, 1963.

Howe, Irving. "A Man of Letters." In *Celebrations and Attacks: Thirty Years of Literary and Cultural Commentary,* pp. 221–24. New York: Harcourt Brace Jovanovich, 1979.

Hyman, Stanley Edgar. *The Armed Vision.* New York: Knopf, 1948.

Josephson, Matthew. Review of *Axel's Castle. Saturday Review,* March 7, 1931, p. 642.

Kazin, Alfred. *On Native Grounds.* New York: Reynal and Hitchcock, 1942.

Kazin, Alfred. *The Inmost Leaf: A Selection of Essays.* New York: Harcourt Brace, 1955.

Kazin, Alfred. *New York Jew*. New York: Vintage Books, 1978.

Kempton, Murray. *Part of Our Time*. New York: Simon & Schuster, 1955.

Kermode, Frank. *Puzzles and Epiphanies*. London: Routledge & Kegan Paul, 1962.

Kriegel, Leonard. *Edmund Wilson*. Carbondale: Southern Illinois University Press, 1971.

Lynn, Kenneth. "The Right to Secede from History," *New Republic,* June 25, 1962, pp. 21–24.

Matthiessen, F. O. *The Responsibilities of the Critic*. New York: Oxford University Press, 1952.

McCarthy, Mary. *Intellectual Memoirs: New York, 1936–1938*. New York, 1992.

Meyers, Jeffrey. *Edmund Wilson*. New York: Houghton Mifflin, 1995.

O'Connor, William Van. *An Age of Criticism: 1900–1950*. Chicago: Regnery, 1952.

Paul, Sherman. *Edmund Wilson: A Study of Literary Vocation in Our Time*. Urbana: University of Illinois Press, 1965.

Podhoretz, Norman. *Doing and Undoings: The Fifties and After in American Writing*. New York: Farrar, Straus & Giroux, 1964.

Pritchett, V. S. "Edmund Wilson." *The New Yorker,* December 23, 1972, pp. 75–78.

Raffel, Burton. "From the Uncollected Edmund Wilson." *The Literary Review* 39, no. 3 (Spring 1996):428–434.

Ramsey, Richard David. *Edmund Wilson: A Bibliography*. New York: D. Lewis, 1971.

Samuels, David. "Edmund Wilson and the Public Intellectuals." *The Wilson Quarterly* 20, no. 1 (Winter 1996), 102–12.

Sayre, Nora. *Previous Convictions*. New Brunswick, N.J.: Rutgers University Press, 1995.

Schwartz, Delmore. "The Writing of Edmund Wilson." *Accent* 2 (Spring 1942): 177–86.

Sheed, Wilfred. "Mr. Wilson and the Cold War." *Commonweal* 79 (January 10, 1964): 434–35.

Simpson, Eileen. *Poets in Their Youth*. New York: Random House, 1982.

Trilling, Diana. *Reviewing the Forties*. New York: Harcourt Brace Jovanovich, 1978.

Trilling, Lionel. "Art and Neurosis." In *The Liberal Imagination,* 155–76. New York: Doubleday Anchor, 1950.

Trilling, Lionel. "Edmund Wilson: A Background Glance." In *A Gathering of Fugitives,* 49–56. Boston: Beacon Press, 1956.

Updike, John. Afterword to *Memoirs of Hecate County*. Boston: Nonpareil, 1980.

Vidal, Gore. "Edmund Wilson: This Critic and This Gin and These Shoes." In *United States 1952–1992,* 275–285. New York: Random House, 1993.

Vidal, Gore. "Edmund Wilson, Tax Dodger." In *United States 1952–1992,* 792–796. New York: Random House, 1993.

Wain, John, ed. *Edmund Wilson: The Man and His Work.* New York: New York University Press, 1978.

Warshow, Robert. *The Immediate Experience.* New York: Atheneum, 1972.

Wilson, Rosalind. *Near The Magician.* New York: Grove Weidenfeld, 1989.

Index

The Author

David Castronovo has written several books of criticism, including studies of Thornton Wilder and Richard Yates (with Steven Goldleaf) and volumes on the idea of the gentleman in English and American literature. He has edited *From the Uncollected Edmund Wilson* with Janet Groth and published reviews and essays in *Commonweal, America,* and *Forward.* He is Professor of English at Pace University, New York.

The Editor

Frank Day is a professor of English and head of the English Department at Clemson University. He is the author of *Sir William Empson: An Annotated Bibliography* (1984) and *Arthur Koestler: A Guide to Research* (1985). He was a Fulbright lecturer in American literature in Romania (1980– 1981) and in Bangladesh (1986–1987).